Spiritual Care

A GUIDE
FOR CAREGIVERS

JUDITH ALLEN SHELLY

InterVarsity Press
Downers Grove, Illinois

InterVarsity Press
P.O. Box 1400, Downers Grove, IL 60515
World Wide Web: www.ivpress.com
E-mail: mail@ivpress.com

InterVarsity Press® *is the book-publishing division of InterVarsity Christian Fellowship/USA*®, *a student movement active on campus at hundreds of universities, colleges and schools of nursing in the United States of America, and a member movement of the International Fellowship of Evangelical Students. For information about local and regional activities, write Public Relations Dept., InterVarsity Christian Fellowship/USA, 6400 Schroeder Rd., P.O. Box 7895, Madison, WI 53707-7895.*

Cover photograph: Ronnie Kaufman/Stock Market

ISBN 0-8308-2252-6

Printed in the United States of America ∞

Library of Congress Cataloging-in-Publication Data

Shelly, Judith Allen.
   Spiritual care: a guide for caregivers/ Judith Allen Shelly.
     p. cm.
   Includes bibliographical references.
   ISBN 0-8308-2252-6 (pbk.: alk. paper)
   1. Caring—Religious aspects—Christianity. 2. Caregivers—Religious life. I. Title.

BV4647.S9 S54 2000
259'.4—dc21

                         99-059907

19	18	17	16	15	14	13	12	11	10	9	8	7	6	5	4	3	2	1
15	14	13	12	11	10	09	08	07	06	05	04	03	02	01	00			

Preface

Twenty-three years ago Sharon Fish and I set out to write a book on spiritual care for nurses. Through Nurses Christian Fellowship we had been teaching workshops on the spiritual needs of patients for several years. As nurses began to practice the principles we taught, they found their nursing care revolutionized. Spiritual care enabled nurses to do what they first became nurses to do — serve God and help other people. Nurses also saw their patients getting well faster and finding peace in the face of death. Each time we taught a workshop, nurses asked us, "Where can we read more? How can we share this information with other nurses?" So finally we wrote the book *Spiritual Care: The Nurse's Role*, published in 1978 and revised twice since.

In recent years it has become clear that the time has come for an altogether new book. Nursing and health care have changed. The interest in spiritual care has grown among health care professionals and among churches. A new role of parish nurse has developed. Spirituality has become a hot topic in every sector.

In the "olden days" when we wrote the first *Spiritual Care*, nurses worked primarily in hospitals. Patients often spent several days in the hospital for "tests" or for minor surgical procedures.

Major surgery required stays of a week or more. Nurses were able to spend time with their patients and get to know them. Visiting nurses frequently continued seeing patients at home for months after hospital discharge. These extended visits usually focused on the psychosocial needs of their patients as well as physical ones. There was time to develop relationships and provide sensitive spiritual care.

Today managed care limits hospital stays to a minimum. What was once considered major surgery may now be performed on outpatients. Nursing assistants provide most of the bedside care in hospitals. A host of specialty health care professionals provides specific services: one starts the intravenous drip, another manages the respiratory therapy, another the physical therapy, and still another gives dietary instructions. Home care visits are short and few and may include the same diverse assortment of caregivers. Patients often feel alone and afraid, lost in an impersonal system. Health care professionals also feel dissatisfied with the changes, frustrated by their inability to provide compassionate personal care.

In the midst of the health care crisis, the need for spiritual care has become much more apparent. Research on the healing power of prayer, the value of faith and the effect of religious commitment on mortality rates has piqued the interest of even the most hardened skeptics. Not only nurses, but physicians and other health care professionals, as well as clergy and lay visitors in churches, are asking for a guidebook to practical spiritual care.

A pastor in the Chicago area, Granger Westberg, had a dream of providing comprehensive health care in churches, with spiritual care as the primary focus. This vision eventually grew into the burgeoning parish nurse movement. These nurses in churches, sometimes called congregational care nurses or health ministers, serve in either volunteer or paid positions as health promoters, educators, counselors, advocates and referral agents—but primarily as integrators of faith and health. Their main focus is on the spiritual dimension of health care.

However, in the rush to include the spiritual dimension in health care, spirituality has become many different things. If you asked someone in 1976, "Are you interested in spiritual things?" you could usually assume that the other person would reply from a Christian context. Not any more. Today you will hear about everything from crystals to goddess worship. Spirituality has also been interpreted generically as something apart from religion. As such, it has become a pursuit of self-fulfillment without content. Christian spirituality, on the other hand, seeks a dynamic relationship with the living God.

This book is designed for anyone who wants to offer Christian spiritual care: nurses, parish nurses, physicians, other health caregivers, clergy and lay visitors. It will help you reach out to people with spiritual needs in your church or professional practice, your next-door neighbor or the person sitting next to you on the bus. The basic premise is that all people have the same essential spiritual needs and that those needs are ultimately met in Jesus Christ. However, we do not have to go rushing in to proselytize or to preach; we can gently share the hope that is within us. We offer compassionate presence, prayer, the Word of God, a gentle touch and a message of hope and healing from the context of a worshiping community. Through it all, the power of the Holy Spirit works through us and in us to glorify Jesus Christ and bring us together into the presence of God the Father.

I am grateful to the many people who have contributed to this body of content over the years. Nurses Christian Fellowship has continued to teach and develop the material. Christian health care workers around the world have caught the vision, conducted research and developed creative strategies to care for the spiritual needs of those who suffer. Special thanks go to those who worked with me to refine the book: Mary Thompson, Linda Kunz, Eleanor Edman, Melodee Yohe, Skip McDonald, Grace Tazelaar and Sharon Fish. I am also indebted to IVP editor Linda Doll for her enthusiasm and encouragement along the way.

To protect individuals' privacy, unless a story is footnoted all names are pseudonyms.

Part One

What Is Spiritual Care?

1

Spirituality & Health

M*ary Lou, a faithful member of the church prayer team, seemed* plagued by chronic illness. An automobile accident ten years ago had crushed several vertebrae, leaving her with nagging back pain. A lingering problem with endometriosis gave her constant abdominal pain. Then her blood pressure started rising, responding poorly to medication. Through it all, Mary Lou appeared serene and sweet-tempered.

Although most people in the church knew Mary Lou and deeply respected her for her strong faith, no one knew her well. Shy and reserved, she rarely attended church function other than the weekly prayer meeting and worship service. She explained that the hard chairs were too uncomfortable for her and that she had to watch her diet carefully. However, now that her blood pressure was up, she began to visit the parish nurse regularly to have it checked.

Kathryn, the parish nurse, asked Mary Lou if she would be willing to go through a health assessment with her. Mary Lou hesitated but then agreed. First they concentrated on the physical problems, which were many. It seemed that Mary Lou spent most of her time visiting medical specialists. She took thirty-seven different pills each day, some of them prescriptions but many of them over-the-counter vitamins and herbal remedies. Kathryn carefully listed each medication, intending to make sure there were no potential adverse effects or drug interactions.

Mary Lou's psychosocial history proved just as complicated. Abused as a child, she had been treated for depression sporadically since she was thirteen years old. Her two grown sons had left home soon after graduating from high school. She had not seen either of them for years and had never met her grandchildren. Her husband, Paul, was her only friend, and she felt she was a burden to him.

As Kathryn began the spiritual assessment, she hoped this would be one area of health in Mary Lou's life. But here she began to get to the heart of many of the other problems. At first she hesitated to use the assessment guide.[1] It contained a checklist of spiritual disciplines and practices, including some that were rather unusual. Certainly Mary Lou wouldn't know about most of these practices. However, to Kathryn's surprise, Mary Lou checked almost every one, including swinging a pendulum, meditating on a mantra, consulting spirit guides and a wide array of alternative therapies. Finally Mary Lou looked up and said, "I desperately want to develop my spirituality—if it's spiritual, I've tried it."

Mary Lou is not alone. Recently, I attended a parish nurse support group meeting. Thirteen parish nurses from area churches were sharing how they help people in their congregations deal with stress. Ten of them were using some form of therapy borrowed from other religions or the occult—yoga, transcendental meditation, tai chi, Therapeutic Touch, crystals, herbal therapies, diets and massage techniques designed to balance yin and yang, talking to "angels," worry stones, aromatherapy and various forms of imagery. As they discussed these techniques, they agreed that the role of the parish nurse should be to minister to the spiritual dimension, and they classified these activities as "spiritual." "What else do we have to offer?" one of them asked.

Spirituality is a hot topic today. Almost every magazine, newspaper and television program has featured it recently. The bookstore at the local mall has a section on spirituality five times the size of the religion section. Most of the books in the religion section are on religions other than Christianity. Just what is this spirituality that people are seeking? Why is there such a great interest in spiritual things?

"You have made us for yourself," prayed St. Augustine of Hippo, "and the heart never rests until it finds its rest in you." God created us to be spiritual beings—people who seek after something beyond ourselves to find context for our lives. The apostle Paul, preaching to the Greek seekers on Mars Hill, explained, "From one ancestor he made all nations to inhabit the whole earth, and he allotted the times of their existence and the boundaries of the places where they would live, so that they would search for God and perhaps grope for him and find him—though indeed he is not far from each one of us. For 'In him we live and move and have our being'; as even some of your own poets have said, 'For we too are his offspring'" (Acts 17:26-28).

Our culture's current fascination with *spirituality* should come as no surprise. That's the way God made us. The soul's deep longing to know God is a basic human need. However, the definitions of spirituality in the professional and popular literature today differ widely. We are not all talking about the same thing. Recently there has been a strong movement away from defining spirituality in religious terms. Religion is seen as narrow-minded, rigid and confining, while spirituality is open-minded, creative and freeing. On the other hand, there has been a trend toward investigating other religions, including Buddhism, Hinduism, Taoism, shamanism and Native American spiritualities. A pantheon of other gods has entered the American religious scene.

Recent polls seem to bear out these observations. A 1997 Yankelovich Partners poll showed that significantly more Americans are dabbling in spiritualism, astrology, reincarnation and fortunetelling than did in 1976 (see figure 1).[2] The Gallup polls, which have been tracking Americans' religious beliefs for more than fifty years, have consistently found that over 90 percent of those polled say they believe in God. However, in 1976 the question was changed to "Do you believe in God, or a universal spirit?"

In 1992 the question was broken down, with some interesting results. While all but 2 percent believed in some sort of spirit, God or life force, only 83 percent claimed to believe in a personal God. Further questioning of this group revealed a "dazzling array of New Age spiritualists who were 'significantly more likely than those who believed in God . . . to say they believe in such things as astrol-

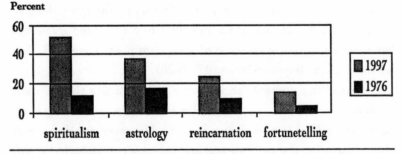

Figure 1. Spiritual beliefs in the United States

who believed in God . . . to say they believe in such things as astrology, ESP, psychic or spiritual healing, déjà vu, ghosts, visits to earth by extraterrestrial beings and reincarnation.'"[3] However, the division between those who believe in a personal God and those pursuing other spiritualities is not clear-cut. If 83 percent say they believe in a personal God, but 52 percent believe in spiritualism, a significant portion of those believers are dabbling in other beliefs as well.

The apostle Paul observed the Athenians' serious pursuit of a vast array of gods and spiritualities in Acts 17. Then he went on to explain that he could tell them about the Unknown God they were seeking. Our own culture's fascination with spirituality presents us with a similar challenge. But we need to be sure we know what kind of spirituality we should be pursuing! In this book, we will view spirituality as *the whole person in dynamic personal relationship with God.* When we compare that to the definitions in recent literature and the communications media, we may find ourselves in conflict. Part of the problem comes from the fuzzy reasoning we experience as we find ourselves floundering in the midst of shifting paradigms and clashing worldviews.

Spirituality and Worldviews

The *modern* worldview comes to us out of the Enlightenment, a movement beginning in the seventeenth century that initiated the modern period of European culture. Although it had its roots in Protestant Christianity and was strongly influenced by pietism, empirical science replaced God as the primary authority. Rationalism, materialism and democracy characterized Enlightenment thought. Most of us have been so immersed in this worldview that we don't realize how deeply we are influenced by it. We assume that if we can't prove something by empirical research, it isn't real or true. God, though usually acknowledged by modernists, is seen as distant, benign and disengaged from the world. Spirituality, for the most part, is viewed as superstition, and religion as a private matter that shouldn't be discussed in intelligent company.

While the modern worldview set the stage for science and technology to flourish, people increasingly began to realize that something was missing. Modernism separates the mind from the body and does not leave room for interrelationships between emotions, beliefs, environmental influences and physical health. On the other hand, it has contributed amazing advances to health care. None of us would want to return to premodern days—before antibiotics, immunizations, anesthesia or modern surgical techniques. But there is a new movement afloat today.

The *postmodern* worldview has begun to replace the modern worldview. It grew out of an attempt by twentieth-century philosophers to *deconstruct* the assumptions of the Enlightenment and modernism. The effects of postmodernism now permeate many aspects of our culture, and it has radically transformed the prevailing understanding of spirituality. The trends in recent literature show a spirituality increasingly devoid of content and divorced from religious faith. It is based in experience—feelings and techniques. Many are quick to explain that "this isn't religious." Consequently, this spirituality is open to everything, for there is no absolute standard of truth. Any spiritual practice that brings comfort, strength or apparent healing is considered equally good and can be incorporated into health care.

To some extent we have all become enculturated into postmodernism, which values tolerance, "political correctness" and multiculturalism. We hesitate to offend people by being judgmental— almost to the point where we don't make ethical distinctions. Although we may think that our Christian beliefs are right for us, we may also consider other religions equally valid and true. Interest in evangelism and missions is waning. Many Christians have forgotten that the gospel is *good news* and that the Bible insists that following other gods will lead us into bondage.

The biblical worldview looks at spirituality differently from either modernism or postmodernism. Actually, the term *spirituality* doesn't appear in the Bible at all. God doesn't tell us to develop our spirituality, because the spiritual is always personal in the Bible. We develop spiritual *relationships*, and we are given a choice—either to accept God's offer of a relationship with him through Jesus Christ or to turn to other spirits. The spiritual world is *real*, not a psychological projection or a primitive superstition. It is not a neutral world. God has warned his people repeatedly to avoid colluding with any other spirits (gods), not because he wants to limit our freedom but because it is dangerous. These spirits are enticing, deceptive and manipulative; "even Satan disguises himself as an angel of light" (2 Cor 11:14).

Too often we approach spirituality from the worldviews that have shaped us, rather than from a biblical worldview. We are pragmatic modernists when we rationalize that we should not talk about religion—particularly Christian witness—in public. On the other hand, we are relativistic postmoderns when we assume that we should encourage any kind of spirituality, seeing it as benign or even good.

As we look at the prevailing trends in spirituality, we need to keep firmly rooted in the solid grounding of Scripture, for it is only God who heals us and satisfies that deep spiritual longing within us. If we truly hope to meet the spiritual needs of those in our care, our spiritual care must be focused on bringing people to Jesus so they can experience that healing personally.

How Does Spirituality Affect Our Health?

The research shows that religion is good for your health. Recent medical research at respected institutions such as Harvard and Duke has appeared in both the professional literature and the popular media. It indicates that regular church attenders live longer; have a lower risk of dying from arteriosclerosis, emphysema, cirrhosis of the liver and suicide; and recover faster when they do get sick. Their diastolic blood pressures are lower than nonattenders, their mental health is better and their marriages are more stable. Furthermore, studies show that prayer "works."

Christians are expressing delight over current medical research on prayer that seems to prove what we have known all along. But here we must exercise caution over our faith in science. Does research prove or disprove God? How can we measure God-at-work? Does prayer work only if we get our way? God wants us healthy and instructs us to pray for healing, but he doesn't answer according to our criteria.

The real question we need to ask is *What does the Bible say about health and healing?* We will examine several biblical concepts. First, the definition of health in the Bible is holistic and broad. It has more to do with healthy relationships than with the absence of disease. Next, healing was a major focus in the ministry of Jesus. Finally, Jesus instructed us to "go and do likewise."

The biblical understanding of health is closely linked with the Hebrew concept of *shalom*. Often translated as *peace*, it is much more than an absence of conflict. *Shalom* refers to a God-centered community where people live in good relationship with their neighbors, caring for one another's physical, emotional and spiritual well-being, economic welfare, social interaction and environmental safety. There is a strong relationship between *shalom* and righteousness. That righteousness is found only through a faithful relationship with God. A righteous life leads to *shalom* and results in joy and flourishing (Is 49:17-20; 51:11-16).

The biblical concept of health is also closely related to the concept of salvation, for the goal of salvation is to bring us into the *shalom* of God (Is 53:4-6; 61:1-4; Jn 14:27). The Greek word *sōzō* means both "health" and "salvation." We see examples of this in Matthew 9. First Jesus healed a paralytic by forgiving his sins; then he demonstrated that healing had occurred by telling him to get up and go home. Then a woman who had suffered with a hemorrhage for twelve years touched the fringe of Jesus' clothing, believing he would heal her. He turned to her and said, "Your faith has made you well *[sōzō]* (Mt 9:22). In both of those situations, the persons healed found more than relief from physical symptoms. They were restored to the worshiping community. They received both salvation and physical healing.

Linsey provides a contemporary example of this holistic healing. Grossly overweight, Linsey's blood pressure soared far above safe levels. Medication did not adequately control it, and a battery of tests could not locate a physiological cause. Linsey also suffered numerous other health problems and seemed unable to lose weight. While praying with a friend one day, Linsey remembered some serious problems from her childhood that had left her angry with God. She was able to picture the scenes in her mind and see Jesus present with her through the terrifying situations. As she began to sense God's love and care for her, she suddenly began feeling better physically and to steadily lose weight. Her blood pressure gradually returned to normal.

Many people would simply say that Linsey's health problems were "in her head." Jesus would probably say that they were in her heart (Mt 13:15). However, that does not negate the reality of the physical symptoms, nor does it indicate that all physical illness is caused by sin. The point is that we cannot separate people into body, soul and spirit (or any other compartments), dividing the aspects among various specialists. While doctors, nurses, counselors and clergy may each focus more intensely on one dimension, all have to work together toward healing. Health and salvation are ultimately flip sides of the same coin.

Some Christians are convinced that the role of the church is to deal only with "saving souls." They fear that too much involvement in social issues might divert us from a concern for salvation. However, salvation and healing are both social issues. True health means living in dynamic relationship with God as fully functioning members of the body of Christ. Jesus never separated health and salvation. Throughout the Gospels we see Jesus teaching, preaching, healing and casting out demons—all at the same time (Mt 4:23-25). Through his healing ministry Jesus verified that he was truly the Messiah (Mk 2:10; 3:11; Jn 11:4).

People flocked to Jesus because he offered healing for physical illness. Often it was only after their physical needs were met that they began to understand Jesus' message. Consider the story in John 9 of the man born blind. At first even the disciples did not treat him with compassion, but merely as an object lesson. The Jewish leaders believed that all suffering was caused by sin, and apparently the disciples did too. However, through his healing, Jesus made the man a much greater illustration of his love.

First, Jesus delivered the verbal message: "I am the light of the world" (Jn 9:5). He was talking about his power to bring salvation. Then he demonstrated his power by applying mud made with his own sputum to the man's eyes, resulting in his healing. The man's faith then grew as he related to Jesus. The man demonstrated his initial faith in Jesus by going, as directed, to wash in the pool of Siloam. When he returned seeing, he immediately came up against opposition from the religious leaders. He fearlessly gave his testimony, calling Jesus a prophet. The attacks on him continued, but he refused to back down. As he defended Jesus to the authorities, his faith and understanding grew. Finally, he encountered Jesus again, asked questions to more fully comprehend who he was and what he had done, then confessed Jesus as Lord and worshiped him. His healing was complete—he could see both physically and spiritually—and that healing restored him to his rightful place in society.

Jesus' death and resurrection made this healing available to all of us. Isaiah tells us: "But he was wounded for our transgressions, crushed for our iniquities; upon him was the punishment that made us whole, and by his bruises we are healed" (Is 53:5). However, we live in a "now and not yet" kingdom. Jesus won the victory over sin, death and Satan on the cross, but we still wait for his return to reign in that power. This time of waiting may be filled with pain and suffering, but even now we experience glimpses of God's promise of healing (Rom 8:18-25). In the meantime Jesus gave us a mandate to care for the sick and needy (Lk 10:9, 37).

The early church took this command seriously. They cared for others, not only for the church members (e.g., Acts 6), but also for believers they did not know (e.g., 2 Cor 8) and those outside the church (e.g., Acts 2; 1 Tim 6:18; Jas 1:27). Throughout church history we see a pattern of reaching out to the total needs of people, intertwined with the proclamation of the gospel. Christian missions have always moved forward with a two-pronged approach, bringing health care to people in other cultures along with the gospel message, so they might experience the healing power of the gospel.

What Is Spiritual Care?

We have established that we are whole people who cannot be separated into unrelated components. So why must we talk about *spiritual care* as a specialized aspect of ministry? Although we cannot divide the person, we can make distinctions. There are different aspects to who we are and how we relate to the world.

We have physical bodies that define us. Paul tells us:

> There are both heavenly bodies and earthly bodies, but the glory of the heavenly is one thing, and that of the earthly is another. There is one glory of the sun, and another glory of the moon, and another glory of the stars; indeed, star differs from star in glory. So it is with the resurrection of the dead. What is sown is perishable, what is raised is imperishable. It is sown in dishonor, it is raised in glory. It is sown in weakness, it is raised in power. It is sown a physical body, it is raised a spiritual body. If there is a physical body, there is also a spiritual body. (1 Cor 15:40-44)

Our bodies are extremely important. We are to care for our bodies (Eph 5:29) and for the physical needs of others (Lk 10:37) but not be obsessed with them (Mt 6:25). They are the temples of the Holy Spirit and a means for glorifying God (1 Cor 6:19-20). There is something beyond the physical body that is eternal. It is that aspect of the person that maintains our relationship with God throughout life and after death. God has been involved in shaping our bodies and every other aspect of our lives from the beginning (Ps 139; Is 43:1). He knows the emotional baggage that we carry and has walked through it all with us (Is 43:2). Our physical bodies, our emotions and our human relationships all interrelate, but there is something more (Phil 3:20-21; 1 Thess 4:13-18). It is the spiritual dimension that ties all the loose pieces of our lives together (Ps 16:8-9; Is 55).

That spiritual dimension is not a separate part of us, hidden deeply within our bodies, that flies away after death. Nor is it a vague, impersonal energy field that merges with the universe. It is the essence of who we are as persons, and it is centered in our relationship with God. The spiritual is always personal.

Spiritual beings—whether God, angels, demons or humans— have wills, intentions and character. Therefore, spiritual care involves facilitating relationships. Christian spiritual care focuses on helping others to establish and maintain a dynamic personal relationship with God by grace through faith. That is made possible through the death and resurrection of Jesus Christ and the work of the Holy Spirit. We serve as ministers of that grace and as representatives of the body of Christ, the church.

As our culture becomes increasingly pluralistic, for some people spiritual care may also mean facilitating relationships with other spirits. Christians need to be aware that for us to do so would be leading people astray. There is no such thing as "generic" spirituality. For a Christian to enter into a relationship with any spirit other than God is idolatry. To lead or even support others in questionable spiritual practices is to be a stumbling block to their faith. For this reason, we must also be careful about where we seek our spiritual direction and guidance. We should not be looking for spiritual techniques or healing practices from other belief systems. Many alternative/ complementary therapies fall into this category. The first rule of spiritual care should be the same as for any medical intervention—*do no harm*. Although these therapies may look harmless and inviting, before using them we must first investigate their spiritual sources and ultimate ends, as well as their safety and effectiveness.

Spiritual care for the Christian includes only those approaches that will deepen and enhance a person's relationship with God. It includes worship, compassionate presence, prayer, Bible reading, a vast treasure store of Christian literature, human touch, music and the love and support of the Christian community.

Spirit Touching Spirit

Why is spiritual care so important? First, because illness, emotional trauma and simple discouragement can cloud our relationship with God. A person in crisis is vulnerable and often desperate. Without the support of caring Christians, anything that promises to help will seem attractive. King Saul turned to a "medium at Endor" (1 Sam 28:7); Mary Lou turned to "spirit guides." Others try everything from shark cartilage to crystals. Good spiritual care keeps a person safely in the arms of Jesus.

It is not uncommon for people who are suffering intensely to feel that God no longer hears their prayers. Their attention span may be short, or their eyesight poor, so that reading Scripture for themselves does not bring comfort. They may not be able to attend worship services or other church events, so they feel cut off from the fellowship. They may feel helpless, hopeless and alone. Romans 12 instructs us to exercise spiritual care toward one another:

> Let love be genuine; hate what is evil, hold fast to what is good; love one another with mutual affection; outdo one another in showing honor. Do not lag in zeal, be ardent in spirit, serve the Lord. Rejoice in hope, be patient in suffering, persevere in prayer. Contribute to the needs of the saints; extend hospitality to strangers. . . . Rejoice with those who rejoice, weep with those who weep. (Rom 12:9-13, 15)

By doing so, our spirits reach out and touch the spirits of others to encourage them in the faith. We represent Jesus to others. Spiritual care is the responsibility not merely of pastors and church leaders but of every Christian who supports others through illness and crises. It puts our physical care and emotional support into a context of faith and hope.

2

Assessing
Spiritual Needs

Connie had always considered herself a faithful Christian, but when she learned that one of the responsibilities of the lay visitors in her church would be to "meet spiritual needs," she hesitated.

She could understand the need to provide emotional support and meet the practical needs of the people she would be visiting, but weren't spiritual needs the pastor's responsibility? She certainly didn't see herself as an expert in theology. If she was visiting in the name of the church, wouldn't that be spiritual enough?

On her first visit to Helen, a homebound member, she gained some insights into what spiritual needs might include. At eighty-seven, Helen had been an active member of the church until she broke her hip. Now she was restless and felt isolated. She talked and talked when Connie visited, not wanting her to leave.

"It's not just the people I miss," Helen explained. "Sometimes I feel so far away from God when I can't get to worship services or come to the prayer meetings." Connie urged her to explain further, and Helen continued, "Well, I like being able to pray with other people. It just seems that God hears other people better than he hears me sometimes. Pastor Jessup's sermons always helped me understand the Bible better too. When I read it for myself, I have so many questions. The tapes are okay, but it's not the same. I like the singing and the choir, but most of all I miss the hugs. Nobody ever touches me anymore—church was the only place I got hugs."

Connie asked Helen about her family, only to discover a complex web of anger, bitterness and tension in Helen's family system. Her husband had died six years previously. Two of her sons inherited the family business, but they could not agree about how to manage the finances. A third son, who had moved to another state, received no interest in the business and felt unfairly treated. Helen felt caught in the middle. The sons constantly bickered and came to her, expecting her to choose sides. She finally refused to speak to any of them about anything. Her eight grandchildren, who were all young adults, still visited occasionally, often asking to borrow money that they rarely repaid. She loved them deeply but did not approve of their lifestyles and worried about them constantly.

The longer Helen talked about her family, the more she dropped her cheerful façade and began to tell Connie about the concerns that had been nagging at her since she broke her hip. "I'm just an old lady, and I'm going to die soon. What kind of a legacy am I going to leave behind? Just a bunch of squabbling sons and grandchildren who haven't darkened the church doors since they were confirmed. What do you suppose God thinks of me?"

Connie didn't know what to say. How could she help Helen?

What *did* God think of this situation? How did hugs and family finances fit into spiritual needs? Suddenly she noticed the time and stood to leave. "Helen, I have to go, but let me give you a hug!"

Helen brightened and said, "Oh, you have helped me so much! Thank you so much for coming. Do you think you could say a little prayer before you go?"

Connie fought the desire to hug and run. She sat back down and reached for Helen's hand. She thanked God for their time together and prayed for Helen's concerns, including her family and her desire to leave a legacy that pleased God. Helen grabbed her hand tightly and wept as Connie prayed. "You just don't know how much this means to me," she sobbed.

This was the first time Connie had ever prayed out loud spontaneously. Although she felt awkward at first, she was glad Helen had asked her to do it. The prayer obviously met a need Helen was feeling, but it also touched something deep inside Connie. She felt a new bond with Helen and a shared hope that God would work in this situation.

What Is a Spiritual Need?

Just as understandings of spirituality differ widely, so do the definitions of spiritual needs. Some see spiritual needs as those areas involved with creativity and the arts. Others see them as psychosocial needs—associated with mental health and social systems. A person's understanding of spirituality will determine the resulting view of spiritual needs. However, the Bible presents a distinct picture of spiritual needs.

The foremost spiritual need that the Bible reveals is our need to be in right relationship with God. *A spiritual need is anything required to establish and maintain a dynamic personal relationship with God.* That is why the gospel is *good news*. God loved us so much that he provided for our need by sending his Son, Jesus (Jn 3:16), through whom God "became flesh and lived among us" (Jn 1:14). His love frees us to love others (Jn 13:34; 1 Jn 4:11-19). We are all living lives of quiet desperation, immersed in the results of sin and in need of forgiveness (Rom 3:23). It is through the death and resurrection of Jesus that we find forgiveness for our sin (Mt 26:28; 1 Jn 1:9) and the ability to forgive others (Col 3:13). Further more, we need to have our lives make sense and be purposeful The need to be needed is a spiritual need. We find meaning and purpose through our relationship with God and his people, and through the love and forgiveness we experience from them.

According to Ephesians 1:5-14, not only does God meet our spiritual needs, he overwhelms us with more than we could ever imagine. He gives us a glorious purpose for our lives when we accept the love and forgiveness that God offers us in Christ. That lends deep meaning to every human encounter, every decision we make and even to our illnesses and suffering.

To summarize, all people experience three basic spiritual needs: (1) to be loved and to love in return, (2) to experience forgiveness and extend it to others, (3) to find meaning and purpose in life and hope for the future. Spiritual needs can ultimately be met only by God, but when we receive from him, the benefits overflow into our human relationships. We become channels of God's love, forgiveness and hope. Paul explained to the Corinthians, "But we have this treasure in clay jars, so that it may be made clear that this extraordinary power belongs to God and does not come from us" (2 Cor 4:7). We may be cracked pots, but God uses us anyway.

Spiritual needs may seem elusive. Although we may observe the effects of unmet spiritual needs, they can be difficult to pin down or to measure. Yet there is a deep yearning in the heart of each person to seek God and, in doing so, to find love, forgiveness and hope. Paul explained, "So we do not lose heart. Even though our outer nature is wasting away, our inner nature is being renewed day by day. For this slight momentary affliction is preparing us for an eternal weight of glory beyond all measure, because we look not at what can be seen but at what cannot be seen; for what can be seen is temporary, but what cannot be seen is eternal" (2 Cor 4:16-18). Most people sense, deep down inside, that only the eternal—the spiritual—holds real value.

What Are the Underlying Needs?

When Connie visited Helen, she indirectly discovered that Helen was experiencing all three spiritual needs. She felt cut off from the love of others at church and in her family, and her loneliness hindered her relationship with God. She missed the hugs! She was also embroiled in family controversies that settled into her heart as bitterness. She needed to forgive and help her sons forgive one another. Instead, she had cut off communication. She worried about her sons and their children, and she worried about what God thought of her. Through it all, life began to look futile. She lost hope and the sense that God could fulfill his purpose in her.

The Holy Spirit worked in the situation, prompting Helen to ask for prayer. Connie prayed with sensitivity to the concerns Helen shared with her. It was a move toward wholeness.

To responsibly meet the needs of those in our care, it is important to systematically assess spiritual needs. Most people will not be as open as Helen.

The most natural approach to assessment is simply to keep the three spiritual needs in mind as you talk with a person you are visiting. Ask about relationships with church, family, neighbors—

and God. Follow up on hints that lingering anger or bitterness may be preventing a person from offering or receiving forgiveness. Listen carefully for references to underlying guilt feelings or fear of God's wrath. Discuss hopes, dreams and goals, as well as encouraging reminiscence about meaningful past events and relationships.

The purpose of a spiritual needs assessment is to determine the nature of a person's relationship to God and other people, and to give the person the opportunity to accept spiritual support. While the Holy Spirit or our sanctified intuition may guide us into recognizing spiritual needs in some cases, we can't rely on that. Sometimes a more formal approach to assessment will enable us to recognize deeper needs that may not be evident in casual conversation.

Observation

The first step in assessment is observing the person and the context that surrounds the person. Use your eyes and ears to find clues about spiritual concerns.

Look around the room. Is the television on? Is it tuned to a worship service or the soaps? Is it just background noise, or does the person you are visiting have difficulty taking her eyes off of it long enough to talk? Is a Bible or other religious literature handy? Does it look as if it has been read much? What other reading material is lying around?

Notice the pictures displayed. If you see religious art, what does it seem to convey about God? Does the room seem warm and inviting or stark, uncomfortable and disheveled? Do you see any odd objects? For instance, when one pastor visited a church member, he noticed several small pyramids prominently placed near the woman's favorite chair. When he asked about them, she explained that her son had made them for her and they conveyed spiritual power. She then invited him to join her in sitting inside a large pyramid in the basement. As he politely declined, he was able to turn the conversation to her understanding of God.

Explore the things you observe. Ask about the people and places in photographs displayed. See if there is a special memory attached to particular pictures. Ask about specific reading material, favorite Bible verses, devotional guides. Inquire about the history behind a unique piece of furniture or decor. For example, asking about an antique pump organ in Henrietta's living room led her to reminisce about playing that same organ in the church when she was a teenager. The good memories were clouded by the time she was reprimanded by an elder for playing popular tunes on the organ after church. She stayed away from church for many years and bought the organ at an auction decades later.

Note affect and attitudes. Does the person appear lonely, depressed, angry, anxious or agitated? If so, is he or she on medications or receiving counseling to help—or might that be contributing to the problem? The side effects of some medications can cause mood swings or depression; chronic depression can often be helped considerably by antidepressants. On the other hand, some depressions can be triggered by unrealistic guilt feelings or fear of God's punishment. Don't assume that every emotional problem has a spiritual component, but don't rule it out, either.

Be alert to behavior that might indicate spiritual need. Does the person appear to pray before meals or at other times? Does he or she read religious literature? Does sleep seem to be a problem? Does he joke inappropriately? For example, on the night before his open-heart surgery, Harold began telling jokes about hell and remarking that he might go there—a loud cry for spiritual help!

Listen carefully. Often people will throw out subtle clues that they want to talk about spiritual things, but they aren't sure how you will respond. Does she mention God, prayer, faith, church or religious topics (even briefly)? Does he want a visit from the pastor? Does she express fear of death? I once cared for a postoperative patient in the hospital who kept putting on his call light to ask for cough syrup. Finally, he said, "I keep coughing and coughing. Do you think I might die?" I could have merely assured him that his trachea was just irritated from the breathing tube used during surgery, but something made me explore further. It turned out that he was afraid that he had lung cancer (which he did not), because he thought God was punishing him for being unfaithful to his wife.

Notice interpersonal relationships. How do family members interact? Who visits? How does the person respond to visitors? Does the person appear to be a loner? If so, does that seem to be a deliberate choice or the result of poor interpersonal skills? Could the person be a victim of emotional or physical abuse?

For example, after suffering a mild stroke, Myrtle moved in with her son and his family. A sweet, quiet woman, she had faithfully attended worship services and a women's Bible study for years but stopped when she could no longer drive.

Jen, the parish nurse from her church, visited weekly, but Myrtle seemed like a different person in her son's home. The family members were loud and inconsiderate of one another, often shouting obscenities. The house was thick with cigarette smoke, to which Myrtle was allergic. Myrtle's room was an unheated back porch that had been enclosed. The only bathroom to which she had access contained a toilet and sink but no bathing facilities. Her eyes were red and watery, and she coughed constantly. Jen offered to take her to the doctor. On the way, Myrtle poured out her story of emotional abuse, explaining that her son had tricked her into signing over the house and her bank account to him. Suddenly Myrtle stopped talking, telling Jen she feared reprisal if her family discovered she was talking. Then she continued, "Why does God allow this to happen?"

Interpreting

The next step in the assessment process is discovering the meaning behind your observations. Observations can be deceiving. They need testing. For instance, Carla and Anna, unmarried sisters who lived with their mother, Edna, appeared to care solicitously for Edna when she became chronically ill. Others in the church openly admired their dedication. However, one day Carla and Anna were away when Mary, the parish nurse, visited. Mary commented on how kind the sisters appeared. Edna's face darkened and she replied, "They're mean to me!" Mary probed gently, asking for more details. "Well, when I don't move fast enough, sometimes they hit me," Edna explained, slowly raising her sleeve to reveal a large bruise.

Asking open-ended questions about items surrounding a person may reveal surprises or allow for further discussion. For example, you could remark, "I see you have a well-used Bible on your coffee table. Do you have a favorite passage?" One person may use that as an opportunity to share the comfort a particular passage has provided, while another may explain that the Bible belonged to another family member who had used it to judge and condemn.

Mary Sue, a part-time youth worker in a neighboring church, frequently referred to her "prayer closet" when I visited, explaining that Jesus commanded us in Matthew 6:6 to go into a closet to pray. It never occurred to me to ask to see the prayer closet. One day she offered to show it to me. As she opened the door, the thick smell of incense filled the room. Inside the closet she had placed a large pillow on the floor facing an altar with candles and a cross—along with an incense pot, a string of Muslim prayer beads, a rosary, and statues—of Buddha, Vishnu and an assortment of unfamiliar idols. Sheepishly she looked at me and said, "I've always been one to hedge my bets."

After taking a few minutes to regain my composure, I asked Mary Sue to tell me about the prayer closet. She related a story of her long spiritual journey and the friendships she had made along the way. Although raised in a Pentecostal church, she became embarrassed by her background while she was in college. She didn't like the restrictions and was eager to see what the "real world" offered. Whenever she met someone she admired, she inquired about their spiritual understandings and incorporated their beliefs and practices into her own, assuming she could remain a Christian. What she really wanted was spiritual power, and these other gods seemed to offer it to her. However, recently she had experienced some frightening encounters in the prayer closet, and she suspected that God was out to get her.

"Tell me more about these experiences," I prompted. What she then described did not sound like an encounter with God. I asked if we could get together the following week for a Bible study. She agreed, and we began with Genesis 3. She immediately saw herself in the story of Eve's temptation in the Garden of Eden. She dropped to her knees in tears, confessed her sin and then dumped all the contents of her prayer closet into the garbage.

No one, including me, had thought to assess the meaning of Mary Sue's unusual prayer life. It sounded biblical, though a little quirky. We took it at face value. Yet her prayer closet was a desperate cry for help, which we ignored. In the meantime, she was influencing her youth group to explore dangerous spiritual paths, leading them astray.

On the other hand, Cass presented another picture. She moved into a new home with her boyfriend in our family-oriented community. She did not expect the neighbors to approve of her lifestyle. Appearing cocky and self-assured, she welcomed visitors eagerly—until any mention of God or church came into the conversation. I assumed the topic was closed. One day after my family and I helped clear the snow from her driveway, she asked what kind of nursing I did. After I explained that I worked for Nurses Christian Fellowship, she eyed me knowingly and said, "I knew it! You remind me of my best friends in nursing school. They were all born-again Christians—and they are still praying for me." That was the beginning of a series of approach-avoidance conversations in which she would bare her soul, then avoid me for months. She did not become a Christian before she moved away, but I'm sure the "Hound of Heaven" is still pursuing her.

The moral of the story is this: We cannot assume that what we observe on the surface is really what is going on in a person's soul. The most pious church member may be sitting in pyramids or hiding ceramic gods in the closet. The foul-mouthed rebel may be desperately seeking God. If you are caring for someone as a nurse, pastor, church visitor or mentor, it might be helpful to work though a written spiritual assessment guide to clarify spiritual resources, needs and concerns.

An assessment guide provides a review of the strength and meaning of a person's religious practices that can open doors to helping the person establish and maintain a dynamic personal relationship with God. This is not a time to make judgments or give instructions; it is simply a time to gather information. You will then be able to intervene more specifically at the person's level of faith and understanding. The questions in table 1 may be useful in gathering enough information to enter the other's religious world as a helping person.[1] In chapters four through eight we will look more specifically at what to do with the information gleaned.

A. To understand a person's beliefs about God	1. How would you describe God? 2. How did you learn about God? 3. How is God involved in your life?
B. To determine the person's involvement in religious practices	1. What spiritual practices have been important to you? Tell me about them. 2. Have you always belonged to the same church? Tell me about your religious history. 3. How has your health affected your involvement with the church? 4. Who are the people who have most influenced your faith?
C. To assess the person's spiritual resources	1. How does your faith help you? 2. Is prayer important to you? How? 3. Is the Bible or any other religious book helpful to you? How? 4. Have any events or experiences changed your feelings about God? How? 5. Has your present [illness/crisis] made any difference in your faith? How? 6. Who are the people who support you spiritually?
D. To assess whether the person's resources for hope and strength are reality-based	1. In what ways is your faith important to you right now? 2. What helps you most when you feel afraid or alone? 3. Is there anything you are hoping for right now? Tell me more. 4. What are your sources of strength right now?
E. To offer the person an opportunity to accept spiritual help	1. What can I do to support you in your faith? 2. Would you like me to pray for you or read the Bible to you? 3. Would you like a visit from the pastor or others from your church? 4. Would you like to receive worship tapes or written materials from the church?

Table 1. Assessing needs

A Self-Assessment

In order to accurately assess the spiritual needs of others, we need to be aware of our own. As we have already determined, spiritual health is closely tied to our relationships with God and other people. The following assessment guide is designed to help you examine your relationship with God in the context of your human relationships.

First, think through the following questions on your own. You may want to write your answers in a notebook or journal. As you write, think about the memories these questions stimulate, and consider areas in your life where you may want to seek guidance or support in making changes.

The guide is especially helpful when used with a friend or prayer partner. Find a partner whom you trust. Agree to interview each other. Allow plenty of time—at least a couple of hours for each of you. Feel free to follow up on thoughts, feelings and concerns expressed, to stop and pray, or to take a break if the interview becomes too intense. You may be surprised by what you discover about yourself and about God's work in your life.

Assessment Guide

1. In one paragraph, how would you describe your childhood?

2. Describe your relationships with your parents and siblings—while growing up and now.

3. If you are or have been married, describe your relationship with your spouse or former spouse(s). If you have never been married, describe the most significant "other" in your life and how that relationship developed.

4. If you are a parent, describe your relationship to your child(ren). If you do not have children of your own, who are the significant children in your life? Describe your relationships with them.

5. What were the most significant *positive* events in your childhood? adulthood? Why?

6. What were the most significant *negative* events in your childhood? adulthood? Why?

7. How did you learn about God?

8. In what ways did you experience God while you were growing up?

9. How would you describe God?

10. What were the crisis points in your relationship with God over your lifetime? What issues were involved? How did your relationship to God change?

11. Who was the most significant person in your faith development as a child? as an adult?

12. If married or formerly married, how has your marriage influenced your faith in God? If never married, how has your closest friend influenced your faith?

13. Describe your faith community (your church and other fellowship groups). In what ways has that community nurtured your faith? How has it hindered your faith?

14. What rituals, disciplines or other religious practices have been particularly helpful or meaningful to you? (sacraments, worship experiences, devotional habits, spiritual direction and so on).

15. Where do you find the most support in your relationship to God?

16. What kind of spiritual support do you need at this point in your life? Are you receiving it?

17. Describe a time when you were angry with God. How did you get through that period?

18. How is God at work in your life right now?

19. In what ways is your faith helpful to you in your daily life?

20. How has your faith influenced the major decisions in your life?

21. How has your relationship with God influenced your care for others?

22. What spiritual resources do you draw upon when you feel overwhelmed?

When you are the interviewer, encourage your friend to tell his or her story as the questions trigger memories and thoughts. This is your time to listen, not to add your own comments. On another day, switch roles.

You may also want to use this guide with those in your care. As you go through the questions, take notice of any clues the other person gives about spiritual concerns. Ask follow-up questions that enable the person to tell about his or her personal spiritual journey. After completing the assessment guide, you will probably want to pray together. Be sure to leave the door open for more discussion on any of the areas of struggle. If deep-seated problems become evident in the course of conversation, gently suggest appropriate professional help such as talking with a pastor or counselor.

3

Breaking the Spiritual Care Barrier

Angela *was an old friend who just happened to be in town when I was* preparing to teach a class on spiritual care. Since Angela taught psychiatric/mental health nursing, I decided to ask her advice about my presentation. She looked at my outline and snorted, "What is it with you and this supposedly *spiritual care?* This is nothing but sneaky evangelism!"

"Haven't you ever had a patient bring up spiritual concerns?" I asked tentatively.

"Never!" she insisted. "Patients don't expect a nurse to meddle in their spiritual lives. If they want spiritual care, they'll go to church."

A large part of Angela's avoidance of spiritual care stemmed from her rebellion against God. Early in her nursing career she spent one term as a missionary in Pakistan. Those three difficult years left her broken and angry. She had been running from God ever since. Her own personal baggage left her unable to hear the spiritual concerns of others. Her graduate-school experience in mental health nursing further solidified her sense that spiritual concerns simply grew out of emotional disturbances—and sometimes caused them.

Angela's reaction to spiritual care came from her own personal struggles. Many times caregivers miss desperate pleas for spiritual help simply because the concerns are not obvious. For instance, Jerry appeared composed and confident before surgery. He never indicated that faith was particularly important to him. When his pastor visited, they watched a football game on television together and joked about the underdog winning. The pastor gave Jerry a firm handshake before he left and said he would be praying for him.

As she transferred Jerry to the operating-room stretcher, Diane, his nurse, commented on how nice it was for the pastor to visit. Jerry's eyes misted slightly, and his voice choked as he replied, "Yes, but I wish he could be a real pastor instead of just a pal."

As she wheeled him toward the OR, Diane asked what real pastors do. Jerry hesitated, then said, "Well, I suppose they pray, but it means more when you can hear them do it." Diane offered to pray with Jerry after moving him into the pre-op area. He grasped her hand and sobbed as she asked God to guide the surgeon and help Jerry heal rapidly. "Thank you so much," he responded. "I have been so scared. It really helps to know that people are praying for me!"

The Bravado Barrier

Most of us have been socialized into appearing self-sufficient and emotionally controlled. Illness or other crises may quickly strip away our defenses, as we suddenly realize that we are not in control of our lives after all. Questions begin to nag at us, for if we are not in control, then who is? Spiritual questions often draw people to God, or even strike fear in their hearts. For instance, Rose began attending church when she was diagnosed with congestive heart failure. When she stopped in to talk with the parish nurse about her condition, she explained, "I'm really afraid that I'm going to die, and if I do, I'll go to hell. How can I get right with God?"

However, most people are not as transparent as Rose. They may appear composed and in control on the surface, but may be falling apart inside. For instance, Jane was a third-grade teacher with metastatic breast cancer. She continued to teach throughout her chemotherapy, as well as to care for her husband and three young children. She never discussed her fears, or even the pain and nausea she experienced, not wanting others to pity her. When Rachel, a friend from church, asked Jane if she could pray with her, Jane sank into the nearest chair, saying, "I thought you'd never ask!"

Remember, we are all spiritual beings. We can bury our spiritual needs beneath a veneer of composure, but the needs remain. Deep down inside, most people yearn for spiritual care and support from others. Don't hesitate to offer spiritual care to others when their spiritual needs do not appear obvious. Assess carefully. Keep your eyes and ears open for cues. Avoid pressuring others, but remain available, even when your offers for help are rejected. We are much more likely to err on the side of caution than to be offensive in our expressions of caring.

Even Angela, my angry, cynical friend, eventually came to me after being diagnosed with bladder cancer, saying, "Okay, I'm ready for that spiritual care you're always talking about. I need it now." In the last years of her life she returned to church, joined a small group Bible study and met regularly with a group of friends to pray. She even began to teach others how to give spiritual care.

Providing spiritual care does not come naturally to most Christians. Our fast-paced, task-oriented culture diverts our attention and sways our priorities. The primary barriers to spiritual care include:

☐ Hidden needs. Needs may not appear obvious—either because people hesitate to express them or because we fail to hear them when they do.

☐ Fear of treading on private territory, thereby offending the other person.

☐ Lack of time.

☐ Feeling unprepared or ill-equipped.

We have already looked at several examples of needs not appearing obvious. Now let's look at the other barriers and consider some ways to overcome them.

Treading on Private Territory

Part of the legacy we have inherited from modernism is the idea that religion is a private matter. When I first began my clinical experience as a nursing student, I carried a three-by-five card in my uniform pocket listing the topics I had been taught were appropriate for conversation with patients. On the flip side of the card, I had written: "Inappropriate topics—sex, politics and religion." My instructors feared that such inflammatory subjects might cause our patients undue stress.

Times have changed. We are much more open now about controversial topics. Nurses are sometimes even required to consider the spiritual as part of their needs assessment. Postmodernism tells us that spirituality is important but religion is rigid and divisive. However, beyond asking a person's church affiliation, most caregivers hesitate to discuss a person's spiritual beliefs and concerns. We attempt to separate our Christian beliefs from our public lives, hoping our faith will be revealed through our actions alone.

Jesus didn't give us that option. He tells us pointedly, "Those who are ashamed of me and of my words, of them the Son of Man will be ashamed when he comes in his glory and the glory of the Father and of the holy angels" (Lk 9:26). We see the apostles Peter and John taking Jesus seriously as they confess before their accusers, "Whether it is right in God's sight to listen to you rather than to God, you must judge; for we cannot keep from speaking about what we have seen and heard" (Acts 4:19-20). Later in his life Peter instructed the church, "Always be ready to make your defense to anyone who demands from you an accounting for the hope that is in you; yet do it with gentleness and reverence" (1 Pet 3:15-16).

The keys to spiritual care are gentleness and respect. Perhaps one good reason people object to overtly expressing hope in Christ is that too many Christians have blundered into evangelism like children caring for an injured animal. They intend to do good, but they end up harming the creature further. Few people have been argued, shamed or bludgeoned into the kingdom. Paul assures us, "I am not ashamed of the gospel; it is the power of God for salvation to everyone who has faith" (Rom 1:16). That is good news—news that we dare not keep to ourselves. Even good news, though, needs to be delivered tactfully.

Jesus gave people the option of saying *no* to him. We should offer the same courtesy to people from other religions or those with no interest in spiritual things. While we can share our faith openly with a Sikh or a Muslim, we should not manipulate or coerce. That is *proselytizing,* not evangelism. While many people may seek God openly when they face a crisis, others will turn firmly to the religion they have grown up with. In such cases, we can assist them in finding someone from their faith tradition to support them. However, we can continue our friendship and listen carefully to their faith stories. We can offer to pray for them. Sometimes we can invite them to Christian events and programs where they will learn about Christ. In the process, we enter into dialogue and look for opportunities to gently share our own story

For example, I met Satomi, a Japanese exchange student, on an airplane. We talked off and on during the fifteen-hour flight from Korea. She had left a sick mother in Japan and felt terribly guilty because they had not parted on good terms. She attended a college near my home, so I invited her to come for weekends. Although she never became a Christian, we talked openly about Christianity and her own experience as an agnostic in a Shinto and Buddhist culture. We discussed her family problems and her difficulties with schoolwork. She attended church with us and frequently asked me to pray for her, which I did. She observed that Christians were "good people," so she wanted to be around them, but she could not take that step of faith.

Getting Up Our Courage

Sometimes we are not really ashamed of the gospel or afraid of reprisal should we discuss it openly—we are simply uncomfortable discussing spiritual concerns. It feels too personal and may reveal our frailty. For example, when Henry suffered a serious myocardial infarction, his daughter called his pastor, frantically pleading, "My brothers and I don't know if my father knows the Lord, and we don't know how to ask him!" Her concern took the pastor by surprise. Henry had always been active in the church, faithfully attending worship and a midweek Bible study. He spoke openly about his love for the Lord, but he had never been able to talk with his children about his faith.

Later in the week, the pastor gathered Henry's family together at his bedside. "Henry," the pastor began, "your kids want to know if you know the Lord."

Henry's eyes misted as he reached out to the two standing closest to him. "Yes, I do. I have prayed for you every day of your lives, and deep in my heart I've wanted nothing more than to be able to talk to you about him, but I'm just an old farmer, and I never had the right words. I just figured your mother would do a good job, so I left it up to her." Hugs and tears followed as the emotional barrier came down. Henry experienced healing not only physically but spiritually as well.

The letter to the Hebrews tells us, "Let us hold fast to the confession of our hope without wavering, for he who has promised is faithful. And let us consider how to provoke one another to love and good deeds, not neglecting to meet together, as is the habit of some, but encouraging one another, and all the more as you see the Day approaching" (Heb 10:23-25). Henry's children saw the day of his death approaching and feared it would be an eternal death. How sad it would have been if they did not have the assurance that they would meet again in heaven.

People long to know and be known in the depths of their spiritual being, but many fear rejection if the truth were known. Consider Fran, a former missionary who taught Christian education in a seminary. Strong, capable and opinionated, Fran seemed to measure her worth by how much she could accomplish for God. After returning from a summer mission trip, Fran came down with a mysterious illness that sapped her energy and finally forced her to take a leave of absence. When Ginny, one of Fran's students, came to visit, Fran tried to maintain her professional composure, but Ginny's intuition prompted her to explore Fran's spiritual needs.

"I think I'd be mad at God if I were you!" Ginny suggested. "Here you invest your whole life serving him, and look where it gets you."

Fran paused, then began to sob. "I feel so useless! I'm beginning to think my whole relationship with God was based on what I could do for him. I was afraid to let him do anything for me. I know we can't earn our salvation, but I sure was trying hard to do it. It's so hard to just sit here and trust God to work, but that's all I can do."

Although Fran's admission was painful for both Fran and Ginny, it was the turning point in her healing. Fran began to realize that she needed counseling to deal with long-covered wounds from her childhood and her missionary experience. She began to learn how to receive from others, and she learned new ways of caring. When she finally returned to the classroom, her teaching was enhanced by her experience with weakness.

How can you get beyond the fear factor in meeting spiritual needs? Get started! Once you take the plunge, each step gets easier.

☐ Find a prayer partner. Pray together regularly. Share what you are learning from Scripture and how it applies to your daily life.

☐ Join a small Bible study or prayer group. Learn to share your own spiritual struggles, as well as listening to others.

☐ The next time someone asks you to pray about a concern, ask, "May I pray for you right now?" You can even do that over the phone.

☐ When someone asks, "Why did God allow this to happen?" follow up on the question. You don't have to provide the correct answer—only God knows that. Ask more about what your friend is feeling and how that affects her relationship with God.

But I Don't Have Time!

Jon looked at his assignment for the day and knew it was impossible. Downsizing had reduced the nursing staff to dangerous levels. During morning rounds, Elsie Morris caught Jon by the hand, moaning, "I didn't sleep a wink last night. The pain was awful! Why does God allow me to suffer so?" Jon groaned internally, trying to move on. He assured Elsie that he would bring her an injection for pain as soon as possible and would check with her doctor about increasing the dosage.

Jon had no sooner started up the hall than Elsie's call light beckoned. He ducked back into the room to check on her. "Where's my shot?" Elsie demanded, then continued, "Don't nurses give bed baths anymore? At least you could bring me a basin and towel!" Jon knew that the IV in room 325 was running low, and three other call lights beckoned. Jon assured Elsie that he had not forgotten her and he'd be back as soon as he could.

As he turned to leave, Jon noticed Elsie's open Bible on her bed. He stopped, sat down in the bedside chair and gently remarked, "I notice that you've got your Bible open. Has a particular passage been especially meaningful to you?"

Elsie looked down at her Bible, shook her head slowly and replied, "Reading the Bible has always been important to me, but I just can't seem to concentrate now."

Recalling a passage that had spoken to him during a time of personal illness, Jon reached for Elsie's Bible and offered to read it aloud:

Surely he has borne our infirmities and carried our diseases; yet we accounted him stricken, struck down by God, and afflicted. But he was wounded for our transgressions, crushed for our iniquities;

upon him was the punishment that made us whole, and by his bruises we are healed. (Is 53:4-5)

"You know, God understands how you're feeling. He's been through it himself," Jon commented.

Elsie pondered for a while, "I'd never thought of it that way. I guess he does understand, but I've been too busy being mad at him to realize it." Jon asked Elsie if he could pray for her. Elsie's face brightened as she replied, "Oh, *yes!*" Asked if she had any special requests, Elsie replied thoughtfully, "Well, pray that I can live to get through my daughter's wedding next month."

Jon laid his hand gently on Elsie's arm and prayed, "Dear Lord, we know that you understand what Elsie is going through and that you are in control of all things. You know how important her daughter's wedding is to Elsie, and we ask that she will not only live to get through it, but that she will be pain-free and full of energy. We pray that you will heal Elsie and keep her close to yourself. Help her to know your love and presence right now. Ease her pain. Give her your peace. In Jesus' name. Amen."

Elsie visibly relaxed as Jon prayed. By the time Jon returned with the pain medication, Elsie was sound asleep.

Many nurses use the excuse that they just don't have time to provide spiritual care. Even in less pressured settings than a busy hospital, we tend to think that we are simply too busy to spend extended time exploring a person's spiritual needs. However, as Elsie demonstrated so clearly above, spiritual care may save time in the long run. When the underlying problem is spiritual, medication, surgery or even psychiatric care will not be as effective as they would be when spiritual needs are appropriately met.

The time factor is simply a matter of priorities. We have been socialized to believe that physical needs are the most important, followed by emotional and social needs. We turn to spiritual needs if there is any time left over, but that rarely happens. Jesus turned this set of priorities on its head in the Sermon on the Mount, teaching, "Therefore do not worry, saying, 'What will we eat?' or 'What will we drink?' or 'What will we wear?' For it is the Gentiles who strive for all these things; and indeed your heavenly Father knows that you need all these things. But strive first for the kingdom of God and his righteousness, and all these things will be given to you as well" (Mt 6:31-33).

How can you make time for spiritual care in a hectic schedule?

☐ Put your relationship with God first in your own life. Get up earlier to spend some quality time with the Lord in prayer, meditation and Bible reading. Or find a time during the day when you will be undisturbed. Convince yourself that this time is important—confirm your commitment to God in prayer. You can't offer to others what you do not have yourself.

☐ As you develop a plan for those in your care, put spiritual needs at the top of the list.

☐ When you assess a spiritual need, follow up on it.

☐ When you find yourself thinking, *I don't have time for this,* stop and pray about how the Lord would have you use the time you do have.

I Don't Know How!

Naomi began her new role as a parish nurse in the church where she had grown up. Although she had been a nurse for twenty years and taken a parish nurse preparation course before starting the new job, she felt anxious making her first home visit. However, Violet Jones quickly put her at ease. Recently discharged from the hospital after abdominal surgery, Violet lived alone. Naomi did a quick assessment of Violet's physical condition and asked about her support system for meals, transportation and other activities of daily living. Then she settled in to listen to Violet's stories of her illness and hospitalization. The time passed quickly, so Naomi rose to leave.

"Oh dear," Violet exclaimed, "I misplaced my glasses again. Can you help me find them?" Naomi searched everywhere without success. Finally Violet continued, "I think I lost them in the hospital. What I really miss is reading my Bible every day. Could you read it to me?"

Naomi found Violet's well-worn Bible and daily devotional guide and read the portion for that day. Violet smiled and nodded as Naomi read, then stated authoritatively, "Now we pray. You go first."

Naomi froze. She had been raised in a Christian home and prayed with her parents as a child, but she did not know how or what to pray with Violet. She began praying the Lord's Prayer, but Violet wasn't satisfied. "You have to talk to God like he's your friend, not just recite things by rote!" she insisted. A long silence followed. Naomi knew Violet expected her to continue, so she nervously added, "Lord, bless Violet and help her get well."

Even Christians who are comfortable praying in a familiar small group, or with friends, may feel awkward about praying or sharing spiritually in a caregiver setting. At one point I worked on a unit with four other Christian nurses. They talked freely about their church activities and Bible study groups, but none of them felt comfortable providing spiritual care. Finally Sue, a pastor's wife, asked if I would teach them how. We met briefly after work for several sessions to go over the basic principles of spiritual care.

Sue's "final exam" came one day when she was cleaning a tracheostomy tube. The highly anxious patient kept choking and blowing the clear plastic tube out of the tracheostomy. When the tube blew out into the sheets for the third time, it seemed to become invisible. The patient began to wheeze. Sue panicked. Then she collected herself and said firmly, "We have to pray about this!" She prayed aloud at the bedside for guidance. The patient relaxed, and the trach tube suddenly appeared in the sheets between her knees. Sue confidently replaced the tube, which slid into place easily now that the patient was relaxed. She emerged from the room triumphantly, marveling at God's intervention. She looked at me, laughing, and said, "I don't know why I didn't start doing this years ago!"

Even pastors may not know how to offer sensitive, effective spiritual care. I once worked in a hospital where the chaplain prided himself on visiting every patient daily. He would stand in the doorway, mutter an unintelligible prayer, then move on to the next room without even acknowledging those in the room in a personal way. New patients would often ask me, "What was that?" They were not comforted.

Spiritual care in a health care context involves extending the worshiping community to people in difficult circumstances. Illness alters a person's status in that community, often making both the sick person and the church members unsure of how to maintain their relationship. For example, Pastor Paul Harris suffered a stroke that left him paralyzed and mentally handicapped. When friends from his former church visited him at the nursing home, he often called them by the wrong name and cried when they told him news they thought would please him. They assumed that their visits upset him, and so they stopped coming. Even the area clergy eventually stayed away. His former colleagues felt awkward around Paul. They simply did not know what to say or do.

Spiritual care does not come naturally. Even after breaking through the emotional barriers to discuss spiritual concerns, most people—including health care professionals and clergy—do not know how to proceed. The knowledge base required goes beyond a basic grasp of Christian doctrine and an understanding of counseling techniques to an integration of the two. Spiritual care in crucial human situations requires us to extend the worshiping community to those who are not able to fully participate in the normal life of the congregation, as well as to demonstrate the faith-health connection throughout the life span.

Offering our compassionate presence means learning to listen carefully and respond constructively, in ways that are consistent with what we believe about God. Spiritual support involves praying and sharing Scripture appropriately, along with offering further resources such as literature, music and touch. Caring for people spiritually also involves helping them consider the spiritual aspects of alternative therapies, as well as whether they might be safe and effective.

The following chapters will give you practical guidance on how to provide effective spiritual care. However, "book learning" is only the first step. Skill comes from practice. The sooner you take the plunge to get started, the more it will become a natural part of your caring relationships.

Several strategies will make this step easier:

1. Find at least one friend or colleague to read this book with you. Discuss what you are learning. Practice on each other. Use the spiritual assessment, pray with each other and study Scripture together, discussing its application to particular situations.

2. You might also want to consider starting a small group to go through this book together, then continue as a support group as you begin to apply what you've learned to your ministry of caring.

3. Finding a mentor—someone who is already experienced in spiritual care—will provide an example to follow and someone to guide and support you through the learning process.

4. Helpful tools for examining your spiritual care interactions include journaling, writing verbatims or case studies and discussing what you have written with your mentor or support group.

5. Don't be afraid to get started. The Holy Spirit promises to give us the right words to say (Mk 13:11) and to be our counselor (Jn 14:16-17). The exciting part of spiritual care is seeing God at work, for ultimately it is not us but God who meets spiritual needs. Once you get started, it becomes an adventure in faith and in seeing God's overwhelming love and sufficiency.

Part Two

Doing Spiritual Care

———————

4

The Worshiping Community

————

When *Herb Jacobs, a long-time member of his church board* and choir, suffered several fractured vertebrae in an automobile accident, the congregation rushed into action. The pastor and other board members visited him frequently in the hospital and for several weeks after he returned home. Church members brought flowers, food, a used wheelchair and other needed medical equipment. Cards filled his mailbox. His recovery seemed to go smoothly, and the entire congregation celebrated Herb's return to the Sunday morning worship service several months later.

But Herb, who was still wheelchair-bound, felt a deep sense of loss as the choir began singing the prelude. He wanted desperately to join them. But even if he had been able to attend the Wednesday night practice, climbing the choir loft steps presented a daunting challenge. Going anywhere required major effort.

Herb and his wife, Emily, did not have enough energy for more than one outing each week. Two fellow board members offered to drive Herb to the monthly board meetings, but they became discouraged after one attempt. Herb weighed 285 pounds and needed assistance transferring to his wheelchair. One board member wrenched his back on the first try. They feared injuring Herb or themselves further.

Eventually Herb stopped attending church completely. Emily did not like sitting alone during the worship services, so she stayed home with Herb, watching a worship service on television. Since Herb had attended church after his injury, most church members decided that Herb was not a "real" shut-in, so the cards, visits and offers of support ended. Gradually, Herb and Emily faded from the life of the church entirely.

The choir missed Herb, though, and wanted to include him in their fellowship. At Christmas time they visited him as a group to sing carols, bringing refreshments for an impromptu party. Both Herb and the choir were thrilled by the time together. The following Christmas they visited again—but Herb's condition had deteriorated. Surgery to correct his problem had resulted in a stroke from an embolus to his brain, leaving him paralyzed and unable to speak. Herb no longer seemed like himself. Most choir members felt uncomfortable with him. They decided to discontinue the tradition.

Connection Interrupted

Illness changes a person's status in the worshiping community. When people can no longer attend worship services and church functions, they may quickly become isolated from the rest of the congregation. First Corinthians 12 reminds us that we are a *body,* and we need to look after our weaker parts:

The eye cannot say to the hand, "I have no need of you," nor again the head to the feet, "I have no need of you." On the contrary, the members of the body that seem to be weaker are indispensable, and those members of the body that we think less honorable we clothe with greater honor, and our less respectable members are treated with greater respect; whereas our more respectable members do not need this. But God has so arranged the body, giving the greater honor to the inferior member, that there may be no dissension within the body, but the members may have the same care for one another. If one member suffers, all suffer together with it; if one member is honored, all rejoice together with it. (1 Cor 12:21-26)

What are some practical ways in which Herb's church could have reached out to include and honor him? Complicated, strenuous wheelchair transfers, lugging heavy equipment and the sheer energy required for Herb to get to worship services probably ruled out regular attendance, even with help from others in the church; however, the church could come to Herb.

The choir made a noble effort, but once-a-year choir parties are not the same as regular worship. Many churches audio- or video-tape their services, training volunteers who deliver the tapes to the homebound in how to meet the spiritual needs of those they visit. Some may view the tapes with the family they are visiting, singing the hymns (remember to bring hymnals or song sheets) and even providing communion. Others will stay to talk briefly, offer a prayer and inquire about any help needed, then return later in the week to pick up the tape and visit again.

Perhaps the board could have come to Herb as well, transferring the monthly meetings to his home during the rest of his term as a board member.

Some homebound members can still participate in the regular life of the church by phone. One of my favorite examples is my friend Margaret. A faithful member of the women's Bible study, she desperately missed the fellowship after she became home-bound following a serious illness. One day the pastor suggested that Margaret could help by calling ushers, greeters, readers and other volunteers to remind them of their duties each week. For three years I received cheery phone calls beginning with "What's up?" every time I had a Sunday morning responsibility. Margaret remained actively involved with the daily life of the congregation until the day of her death.

Fellowship is essential for a vibrant faith. I remember once hearing a beautiful illustration of this truth. A pastor was visiting a crusty old member who insisted that he could worship God in his back woods better than by sitting with all the hypocrites in church. The pastor looked into the glowing embers in the fireplace and thought briefly. Then he slowly took the tongs and lifted one coal from the rest, laying it on the hearth. He said nothing, as the two watched the single coal grow cold and gray. The man was in church the following Sunday.

Hebrews puts it this way:

> Let us hold fast to the confession of our hope without wavering, for he who has promised is faithful. And let us consider how to pro-voke one another to love and good deeds, not neglecting to meet together, as is the habit of some, but encouraging one another, and all the more as you see the Day approaching. (Heb 10:23-25)

However, merely physically connecting people to the worshiping community may not be enough. Less debilitating conditions, which may not prevent a person from attending church functions, may separate them emotionally and spiritually from others who appear to be healthy and trouble-free. The church needs to "rejoice with those who rejoice, weep with those who weep" (Rom

12:15). In order to do that, we need to develop skills to recognize who is rejoicing and who is weeping.

Alice came to Carrie, the parish nurse at her church, to have her blood pressure checked. Carrie noted that this was Alice's first visit, so she asked if anything in particular brought her. Alice seemed relieved to have the opportunity to talk. She began, "Well, I just don't feel like I can talk to anyone about this, but my doctor told me I have diabetes, and it can affect my blood pressure, heart and kidneys—and I could even go blind. I'm so *scared!*"

Carrie listened carefully to Alice, asking her to explain further. Alice described how alone she felt. She was trying hard to stick to her diabetic diet and had lost fifteen pounds already, but her husband complained that he liked her chubby. He constantly tempted her with ice cream and potato chips. Her friends told her she looked sick after losing the weight, because her clothes were now too big for her. At first she asked to be on the church prayer list, but so many people asked her embarrassing, intrusive questions that she asked to be removed. Her blood sugar was now controlled by diet alone, so her friends and family considered her cured. She finally decided this was a battle she would have to fight alone, but that was a painful choice.

At Carrie's suggestion, Alice began attending the monthly healing services at church. Having the opportunity to come forward for prayer in a smaller, more intimate service helped her to commit her fears to the Lord. She not only gained the strength to maintain her diabetic diet but also began teaching Sunday school and serving in various volunteer roles in the church. Her whole affect changed dramatically.

Barry also suffered silently. A hard-driving executive, accustomed to being in control of every situation, he was diagnosed with prostate cancer. Although he attended church regularly, up until this point in his life he had never felt the need to depend upon God or other people for anything. Suddenly he felt helpless, fearful and ashamed, but he did not know how to reach out. Turning to God now seemed hypocritical. However, when his name was included in the intercessions during a Sunday worship service, he wept openly.

Everything in our culture drives us toward self-sufficiency and personal independence. The media, health care, educational institutions, our child-rearing practices and our common ethical values regard *autonomy* as the primary goal of maturity and a basic human right. However, that standard only works as long as we are healthy, young, affluent and relatively intelligent. Most ethicists would tick off autonomy, along with beneficence, nonmaleficence and justice as unquestioned standards of ethical behavior. However, the Bible paints a different picture.

The Hebrew community of the Old Testament, which was clearly reflected in the life and teachings of Jesus, held *shalom* as their central operational value. We touched briefly on this concept in chapter one, but it bears further discussion. *Shalom* is seen in a God-centered community in which people relate to one another with faithfulness, integrity, mutual respect and affection. It includes peace, prosperity, rest, safety, security, justice, happiness, health, welfare and wholeness of life. The individual within the community works toward *shalom* through *ṣeḏeq*, Hebrew for righteousness.

Although this righteousness was codified into the Law of Moses, summarized in the Ten Commandments, it is more than a legalistic standard. *Ṣeḏeq* is essentially any action that facilitates *shalom*. To the Hebrew community, righteousness was always connected with delivering, saving and restoring. A righteous person was one who had experienced God's restoration and deliverance, not necessarily one who simply followed the rules. In this context, Jesus summarized the law, God's standard of righteousness, in terms of relationship: "'You shall love the Lord your God with all your heart, and with all your soul, and with all your mind.' This is the greatest and first commandment. And a second is like it: 'You shall love your neighbor as yourself'" (Mt 22:37-39).

Examining the New Testament from this perspective gives us new insights into how the church should function in the world. Jesus told his disciples, "By this everyone will know that you are my disciples, if you have love for one another" (Jn 13:35). That love is demonstrated throughout the New Testament. It includes teaching, healing and caring for one another through illness, adversity, interpersonal conflicts, moral lapses and the whole gamut of human frailties. The church is never presented as a picture of perfection but as a struggling community characterized by commitment to Jesus Christ and to one another, as well as to a deep desire to spread the good news of salvation.

How the Church Shows Care

What would a church look like in today's culture if we were to make *shalom* our primary aim? First, it would require us to reorder our values—to put one another and our life together as a community before our personal quests for power, prestige, wealth and possessions. Second, we would have to drop our façades of independence and self-sufficiency to be vulnerable to one another and support one another in weakness. Third, we would begin to notice the weak and suffering within the church community and to care for them lovingly. Finally, we would reach out in love to the broader community. Let's consider some practical ways we can begin to make those changes.

1. Reordering our values. "I'd love to help, but I'm just so busy right now!" How many times have you heard this excuse for not getting involved in a particular ministry opportunity? How often have you used it yourself? We are so absorbed in the importance of what we are doing that we seldom take the time to pull back and ask God where we should be investing our time and energy. No one can do everything. We are constantly bombarded with the maxim, "You've just got to learn how to say *no!*" However, as Christians, our first concern needs to be where we should say *yes.* When we spend regular time in prayer, meditation and Bible study, as well as periodic times of extended retreat, it becomes much easier to sort through the vast array of opportunities and seek God's direction.

For example, Irene worried constantly about her future. As a single woman in her mid-forties, she felt that she had to carefully prepare for her retirement. After all, she had no one else to take care of her. She worked long hours, with frequent business trips, in a job she hated. The salary and benefits seemed too good to relinquish. Although she attended church faithfully when she was home, she had little time to become involved in other church activities or ministry opportunities. Frequent promotions increased her self-esteem but further impinged on her personal time. Then her father died suddenly of a heart attack. Soon afterward her mother was diagnosed with Alzheimer's disease. When it became apparent that her mother could no longer function at home alone, Irene returned to her parents' home for a two-week visit to assess the situation. She investigated nursing homes in the area, but she also spent a great deal of time reading about Alzheimer's disease, studying her Bible and praying. She also began reconnecting with old friends and her former church community.

With time to reflect in this setting, Irene found her values beginning to shift. She discovered that she had not been trusting

God to provide for her needs. In the process, she had ignored the needs of her family and friends. She decided to take a step of faith—quit her job and move home to care for her mother. Eventually she organized an Alzheimer's support group in the church. It grew to a network of support groups in her metropolitan area. After her mother's death four years later, Irene's involvement with families caring for victims of Alzheimer's disease grew to a full-time ministry. Although the job paid far less than her high-powered position in industry, the rewards were much greater, and she knew God would care for her needs.

Irene's decision may seem drastic. Obviously we can't all quit our jobs to care for aging parents, much less to do full-time Christian ministry. However, we can learn from her example to seek God's direction for our lives and for the time he gives us, so that we can work for *shalom.*

2. Reordering our lives: A guided personal retreat. The prophet Jeremiah offers us some clear direction in sorting through our values and priorities. Take a day when you can go off to a quiet place by yourself to seek the Lord's leading for your life. Allow at least four hours for your retreat. Take along a Bible, hymnal, pen and paper, and a lunch. Begin by committing your time to the Lord. Sing a hymn or two. Next, read Jeremiah 29:1-14, a message to people who were living as captives in Babylon, then meditate on verses 10-14 using the following suggestions.

"This is what the LORD says: 'When seventy years are completed for Babylon, I will come to you and fulfill my gracious promise to bring you back to this place'" (Jer 29:10 NIV). In what ways do you feel that you are in "captivity"? A difficult job situation? Family or relationship problems? Physical limitations? Habits or addictions? Read Psalm 137. Allow yourself to feel the emotion expressed. Let the Lord show you areas of sin in your life and lead you to repentance. Read Romans 7:4-6. Meditate on how God is fulfilling his gracious promises to you. Thank him for it.

"'For I know the plans I have for you,' declares the LORD, 'plans to prosper you and not to harm you, plans to give you hope and a future'" (Jer 29:11 NIV). Read Isaiah 30:1-22 and Isaiah 55. Meditate slowly on each verse, considering the contrast between God's plans for you and your own values and goals. Read Proverbs 3:5-8. Ask him to direct you. God does not reveal the whole future, but he will show us the next step.

"Then you will call upon me and come and pray to me, and I will listen to you" (Jer 29:12 NIV). Envision Jesus sitting with you, perhaps holding your hand. Tell him about all your fears and concerns. Pray for the people in your life who need God's love and direction—friends, family, Christian leaders, missionaries, government and nursing leaders. Read Matthew 6:5-15; Romans 8:26-27; and 1 Timothy 2:1-8. After Jesus has listened to you, be quiet and listen to him.

"You will seek me and find me when you seek me with all your heart" (Jer 29:13 NIV). Now envision Jesus sitting on a throne. Read Isaiah 6:1-8, then Isaiah 57:15. Praise him for his sovereignty and his personal concern for you. Meditate on the character and attributes of God. Read prayerfully John 1:1; 8:12; 10:14; 11:25; 14:25-26; 16:7-15; Colossians 1:15-20; 1 Timothy 1:17; Hebrews 1:1-4; and 1 John 4:15-21. Affirm your love and commitment to the Lord and his people. Praise him for who he is.

"'I will be found by you,' declares the LORD, 'and will bring you back from captivity. I will gather you from all the nations and places where I have banished you,' declares the LORD, 'and will bring you back to the place from which I carried you into exile'" (Jer 29:14 NIV). Read Matthew 7:7-8. Pray for all the people who are involved in or affected by your "captivities"—unreasonable managers, difficult coworkers, supervisees, friends, family members, patients, fellow church members. Envision the "place" God is bringing you into. Ask him to lead you toward it. Read Isaiah 60:1-3 and 61:1-3. Thank him for his salvation (and all that it means in practical terms).

3. Dropping our façades. Bruce and Melissa Tompkins took seriously the biblical injunctions that church leaders should first be able to manage their own households as a prerequisite for leadership. Bruce had served his congregation as their pastor for fifteen years. He prided himself on his strong family values. His teenagers excelled in school and sports. They took active roles in the church youth group and related well to the adults in the church. Then one night their seventeen-year-old son, Brian, was arrested for drunk driving, and the police found marijuana in his car. Suddenly, the Tompkins's lives were thrown into turmoil.

The following evening Bruce faced the church board at their monthly meeting. He knew they would soon hear from others about Brian's arrest. Overcoming deep embarrassment, he decided to share his story with them. Rather than reacting with the anger and blaming that he expected, one by one the board members began sharing their stories of humiliation over their own teenagers' behavior. Several were in the midst of similar struggles. The following day, one of the board members called Melissa, saying, "I need to talk to someone, and I know you'll understand after what Bruce shared last night. Our Mark has been on drugs for several months now. We don't know where to turn. It's something you just can't talk about in church!"

It's something you just can't talk about in church! How sad. The Christian community is the place where we *should* be able to talk about our deepest concerns and find help, but for most Christians it isn't. By trying to maintain a façade, we cut ourselves off from our most important sources of support and strength. The church needs to be a hospital for sinners, not a showcase for saints. We have to revise our understanding of righteousness. Rather than trying to appear perfect in the eyes of others, we must become a community of people who know we have been rescued, restored and forgiven. Then we can reach out in love to others.

4. Reaching those in need. Jesus called us to serve the broader community as well as those within the church. Within our neighborhoods, those who have no church affiliation may be even more alone and needy than people already in the fellowship. Extending spiritual care to the larger community can come through opening congregational health fairs to the general public, visiting homebound individuals referred by friends or relatives, advertising support groups in the local newspaper, providing worship services in retirement communities and extended-care facilities or offering a Sunday afternoon or weekday healing service.

How can we make a start at becoming a caring, witnessing community? Many churches fly into action, trying every innovative program that comes along. Many times those programs fail because they are not appropriate for that particular community or there is a lack of qualified leaders or adequate training. Some churches have so many programs going already that any new program must compete for time in the schedules of leaders and those to whom the program is directed.

Just as we need to assess individual spiritual needs, it is important to begin with an assessment of a congregation's resources and needs before beginning any new approaches. It is important to do your assessment in that order. Starting with needs can lead to either becoming overwhelmed at the immensity of the task or duplicating what is already available. Begin assessing the resources and programs already in place. You may be surprised at how much your church is already doing to reach out to people who are in special need of support. Many times these ministries are hidden, discovered only by word of mouth or reading the fine print in the monthly newsletter.

A Congregational Resource Assessment

1. What is the church already doing in regard to health and caring ministries (healing services, pastoral visits, support groups, teaching, counseling, volunteer services)? Talk to the pastoral staff, the church secretary, board members, deacons, committee chairs and others who may not have official titles but seem to be active volunteers.

2. Who is currently providing these services? What provisions are in place for support, education, reinforcements?

3. Canvass the registered nurses in the congregation, asking about their education, experience and availability. Our congregation keeps a list of nurse members who work in area hospitals and alerts them when a church member is admitted. Many people feel reassured to see a familiar face on the nursing staff, especially if the hospital experience is new to them.

4. List others in the congregation who might be willing and able to help, including physicians, licensed practical nurses, certified nursing assistants, physical therapists, dietitians, counselors, as well as other caring people who spontaneously reach out to others.

5. What does your church library provide? Look for books that relate to faith and health, marriage, divorce recovery, child development, parenting, depression, stress, substance abuse and the like.

6. What resources do your denomination and fraternal organizations provide? Many have books, handouts, conferences, training programs, support groups and networks of people with similar

concerns in other congregations.

7. What are neighboring churches of other denominations providing? Can you network with them to serve a wider community?

8. What community services does your local hospital provide (free screening for blood glucose, cholesterol, skin cancer, gastrointestinal bleeding; educational programs; opportunities for parish nurse education and collaboration; support groups, shelters, counseling, emergency services)?

What Are the Needs?

Once you have surveyed your resources, examine the needs. You can begin by simply observing and talking to a few people. Start with the Sunday-school teachers and church leaders. You could also develop a short survey for a sample group (such as an adult Sunday-school class) to complete. Include the following areas in your assessment:

1. Health education/promotion—congregation-wide information on physical, emotional and spiritual health (knowledge about self-care, diet, exercise, stress, preventive measures)

2. Consultation/counseling—teaching and supporting individuals (visits to home, hospital or long-term facility, posthospitalization follow-up, teaching and supporting family caregivers, making appropriate community referrals)

3. Volunteer services—organizing and coordinating groups and specific ministries (prayer ministry, home visitors, support groups, providing meals for the sick)

Developing a Plan

Start small, but don't try to do it all yourself. Remember that the church is a body with many parts that need to work together. Find several others who share your vision. Think together about how you might be able to meet some of the unfilled needs. You will not be able to meet them all. Match your proposed program with your resources. For example, you may want to start a volunteer parish nurse program, a weight-reduction support group, a visitation ministry to the homebound or a parenting class—but don't try to do them all at once.

Develop a mission statement (your main purpose) and put your goals (the ways you plan to accomplish the purpose) in writing. Consider everything that will be needed to carry out your goals, including a budget. Include such things as training programs and materials, equipment, meeting and storage space, advertising, record-keeping, legal issues, and liability insurance. Decide who will be responsible for each aspect of the project.

Meet with the pastor and the appropriate church leaders for counsel and to gain their approval and support. Then begin recruiting participants. They will usually be able to provide insights into where to find the best response, and often they have the benefit of past history with such programs. While hearing "It's been tried before, but it didn't work" may not be a conclusive argument against trying again, the past experience may reveal some pitfalls to avoid. Now you are ready to begin.

5

Compassionate
Presence

Rosalie felt *duty-bound to visit every hospitalized member of her* church. At first her pastor appreciated her faithfulness and concern, but then reports began to filter back. "I know Rosalie means well," Mary confided, "but I always feel worse after she visits. She tells me all about her own health problems and past operations, and she warns me of every complication that can happen. Please don't let her come again!"

Compassionate presence is more than just showing up at the bedside when a person is sick. It requires us to relate to others as individuals, person to person, without benefit of props. It is *being with* rather than *doing for*. It involves listening carefully to someone who is suffering and responding appropriately to their concerns. To do so we must be willing to become vulnerable and committed to the other person, rather than rattling on about our own opinions and experiences. It requires humility—admitting that we don't know all the answers—rather than coming as an authority. It is not an easy task, for it demands giving of ourselves to others, a task that may leave us feeling drained.

Active listening, empathy, vulnerability, humility and commitment comprise the basic skills we must learn through faith, education and practice. Jesus demonstrated all of these skills in his ministry, as described in the Gospel accounts. Paul summarizes these attributes in practical terms: "Rejoice with those who rejoice, weep with those who weep. Live in harmony with one another; do not be haughty, but associate with the lowly; do not claim to be wiser than you are" (Rom 12:15-16).

The ability to offer compassionate presence to others comes from our faith in God. The first step toward developing a caring presence is to maintain a strong devotional life so that we have something to offer to those in spiritual need. The Holy Spirit working through us will bring comfort and strength to others, but we have to step aside to allow him to work through us. We are constantly tempted to *say something* or to have ready answers to hard questions. Reciting Romans 8:28 ("All things work together for good for those who love God") or telling someone that some sin in their life is causing their problem simply doesn't help. Our role is to set the stage for God to work in a person's life, not to fix the problem.

Faith prepares us for ministry to others, but we also need to learn the specific skills of active listening, empathy, vulnerability, humility and commitment. Furthermore, it will take practice before those skills become second nature. Rosalie, the church visitor in the opening story, had faith, but she lacked the skills to support others in their suffering.

Listening

Listening is an acquired skill. It involves hearing and understanding not only what people are saying but also what they are afraid to say. Careful listening enables you to perceive some of the reasons behind another's verbal and nonverbal communication.

At times unconscious barriers may cause us to use *selective listening*—hearing only what we feel equipped to handle. As we become aware of these barriers (see figure 2), we can begin to overcome them and hear what others are really saying.

Figure 2. Barriers to listening

Word meanings may be a barrier to hearing a person's expression of spiritual needs. Each Christian tradition has a unique vocabulary for describing important aspects of faith and practice. For instance, the terms describing a person's faith relationship with God may differ. "Accepting Christ," "becoming a believer," "getting saved," "being born again," "being baptized" and "awakening to new life in Christ" may seem synonymous to some people; to others only one of those terms may be acceptable. The word *spirituality* itself may mean many different things. Lingo may be a convenient shortcut in communication, but only if you are sure a term means the same thing to the other person as it does to you.

For example, Joann felt alone and afraid when she was admitted to the hospital for tests. However, she felt a flood of relief when she saw a gold cross on her nurse's lapel. She asked the nurse tentatively if she was a Christian. "Yes!" she replied. "I'm a born-again, Bible-believing Christian; are you?" While Joann had a deep faith commitment and spent hours reading her Bible, the terms the nurse used were associated in her mind with manipulative TV evangelists. She retreated into her quiet fear and did not respond.

Preconceptions prevent us from hearing clearly what others are saying. The most overriding preconception affecting spiritual care is the idea that anyone who is truly serious about a relationship with God must believe what I believe and behave as I behave.

For instance, I once cared for a sixty-eight-year-old man whose verbal communication consisted of demands to serve him, delivered with a liberal sprinkling of profanity. One day when I did not respond immediately to his command, he threw the contents of his urinal at me. I was furious and avoided him as much as possible after that. Later, reading his chart I discovered that he was a retired seminary professor. The combination did not seem compatible to me, and I judged him severely in my mind. Several days later, his wife was in the room when he demonstrated similar behavior. I could see tears in her eyes. She followed me out of the room and explained, "He was never like this before. He is a man of God, but after the cancer spread to his brain, his personality changed. I'm so sorry!"

Anxiety creates further barriers to listening. When you are anxious, you focus on yourself rather than on the person in need. Any time we are faced with a new situation or learning new skills, anxiety about the task we are performing may prevent us from hearing the other person. For this reason, we may not become involved in meeting spiritual needs when we are immersed in a new situation. Once we become comfortable with ourselves and the situation, we will be able to hear the other person's expression of anxiety.

Closely related to anxieties are personal *defenses*. When a person offends us or attacks something we hold dear, we tend to put up defenses to protect ourselves and our values. For instance, a person's expression of anger toward God might cause you to respond by defending God rather than hearing the person's cry of desperation. Another person's seductive behavior might cause you to avoid him rather than setting limits and staying to listen.

While it is important to set goals for spiritual care, predetermined *purposes* may also create a barrier to listening. For instance, a church visitor may go to a homebound member's home intending to play the videotape of Sunday's worship service. Realizing that he still has one more shut-in to visit, he may put the tape in the VCR and not hear the person's quiet remark, "My toe is turning black. The doctor says it may have to be removed."

Finally, *values* prevent us from listening with open ears. We are constantly meeting people whose values are different from our own. It is often difficult to feel compassion for someone who has violated our own moral standards and suffered for it. We tend to think that person deserves what he got. For example, a nurse who disapproves of abortion may be unable to listen compassionately to the fears and concerns of a woman undergoing the procedure. Many persons with AIDS have experienced extreme prejudice, regardless of how they contracted the disease.

All of us have certain values that govern our moral behavior. These values arise out of our beliefs, experiences and environment. When we force our values on other people, we unconsciously assume that their beliefs, experiences and environment are the same as our own. To suspend judgment so that we may listen to the hurts, fears and concerns of others may show us that we too might have acted in a similar manner, had we been subjected to the same influences. Listening sensitively does not require us to agree with the other person or condone behavior that violates our moral values, but it does enable us to empathize with people. Through empathy we can become agents of creative change.

Empathy

Empathy is the ability to understand what a person is feeling and to communicate that understanding while remaining objective enough to analyze the situation and provide assistance. Empathy is a process involving both the mind and the emotions.

The first stage in the process is *assessment*—collecting the facts about the person's affect, behavior, physical condition, environment, support systems and so on.

But just gathering the facts does not enable us to truly care. For example, Betty seemed accident-prone. She no sooner recovered from one injury or minor surgery than another occurred. During a church softball game, parish nurse Marty Jacobs watched Betty smash a soft drink bottle against a large rock, then immediately begin picking up the pieces with her bare hands. Marty warned Betty to stop collecting the glass, then went into the church building to find a broom and dustpan. When she returned, Betty sat holding a tissue over a large laceration on her palm. Marty was so annoyed with the dynamics of the situation, and so intent on cleaning and dressing the wound, that she almost missed it when Betty told her, "My husband left me again yesterday. We had an argument, and he hit me."

Suddenly Marty realized that this was more than an offhand comment. As it hit full force, Marty felt a knot forming in the pit of her stomach, and anger welled up at Betty's husband, Wayne. She applied pressure to the wound and looked at Betty. "Tell me what happened." At this point, Marty entered the second stage of the empathy process; she felt *sympathy*. She moved from focusing purely on the facts and the physical situation to sensing the feelings. She also began to feel Betty's pain.

In the sympathy stage we respond as if we were the other person. But if we stop at this point, we can become as immobilized as the hurting person we are trying to help. If Marty had stopped at the sympathy stage, she might have responded, "That rotten snake! How could he do that again? Why don't you just divorce the jerk?" Our inner responses depend on our own background and resources. While Marty's response was to become angry with Wayne and want to retaliate, Betty still loved Wayne and wanted him to come back to her. Had Marty reacted out of her own feelings, Betty would probably have felt that she needed to defend Wayne. Instead, Marty gave her the opportunity to share what she really felt.

At the third and final stage, *empathy,* we put the facts and the feelings together to examine them objectively. In so doing, we begin to discern why Betty feels as she does. Here the focus is back on Betty's needs and feelings. Marty can now support Betty effectively and encourage her toward constructive action. By providing an opening for Betty to talk further about what happened, Marty can understand the situation better and guide Betty toward the help she needs to overcome an abusive marriage.

The process of empathy becomes almost second nature in a sensitive, mature caregiver. But as learners we need to look at the stages to discover where the difficulty lies if our responses do fall short of empathy. If you find yourself remaining cool and aloof with people in need of help, spend some time considering what barriers in your own emotions prevent you from entering into the concerns of others. Thinking back on crises you have encountered, how you felt and what kind of help you wanted at the time may increase your awareness of the feelings and needs of others.

On the other hand, if you find yourself overwhelmed by your concern for others and depressed by their problems, focus on assessment. First, examine the memories and feelings that the other person's situation triggers in you. Write down what you are thinking and feeling. Talk to a close friend, pastor or counselor. Next, discover the resources available to deal with the problems. Spend more time looking at the objective facts. Research the creative alternatives. Read books about people who have endured suffering and overcome serious handicaps to lead meaningful and productive lives. Then you will be more able to move beyond sympathy to full empathy.

Vulnerability

Developing empathy requires vulnerability. To "feel with" another person opens us to the possibility that we too will experience pain. To offer ourselves as a resource to other people creates the likelihood that at some time we will be rejected. Compassionate presence involves lending people our strength until they can regain their own strength. We may feel drained in the process. Caregivers who are vulnerable are those who are willing to open themselves up to rejection, criticism and pain, as well as to the joy and praise of other people, as they respond to people in a caring relationship.

Jocelyn Collins is a good example of vulnerability. Jocelyn volunteered in a church-related women's shelter. Her desire to serve grew out of her experience as a young woman. While she was a college student she had lived with an abusive boyfriend. When she became pregnant, her boyfriend forced her to have an abortion. Afterward he called her a worthless slut, and the abuse intensified.

When she finally began to fear for her life, she left him, finding help in a women's shelter. Now married with two small children, she had moved to a new community and a new church where no one knew her history.

As Jocelyn tried to talk with Kay, a new resident in the shelter, she found herself reeling inside as Kay spewed venom at her. "How could you possibly understand? You're so sweet and innocent. You—with your nice husband and comfortable home! You don't know what it's like to be in this situation."

Jocelyn could see the pastor's wife within earshot. She really did not want to reveal all the ugliness of her past, knowing she would probably have to explain it all over again, but she knew she had to be vulnerable. "Yes, Kay, I do. Ten years ago, I was in a similar situation. I felt so alone and afraid."

Kay's attitude shifted immediately. She poured out her fears, concerns, hopes and dreams—her love for her boyfriend and fear of losing him, and well as her fear of his abuse. "Do you *really* think I can get through this?" she implored.

Jocelyn put her hand on Kay's shoulder, "With God's help, I *know* you can." She continued to visit Kay regularly, simply listening to her and encouraging her, until Kay gained the confidence and financial security to move to another state with her children.

Allowing ourselves to be vulnerable forces us to recognize our humanity. As human beings we *are* vulnerable. We hurt, we fail, we are intimidated by death, we experience pain both physically and emotionally—we need someone to support us as we support others. To function as if we were not vulnerable is destructive to our own emotional health and creates barriers between us and those we want to help. By being honest about her own past, Jocelyn opened a whole new avenue of ministry with others, but she also gained continuing support for herself. When others know the worst about you and still love you, you can live without fear of being "found out."

Humility

Recognizing our own humanity is also an expression of humility. To know we are human is to recognize our limits as well as our strengths. Humility protects us from the temptation to feel omnipotent and indispensable. It enables us to trust others enough to provide aspects of care that are beyond our own expertise. Compassionate presence with another person can develop a bond so strong that eventually a caregiver begins to feel "ownership" of the other person, which then creates a sense of resentment when others attempt to help. At this point our presence ceases to be compassionate and becomes manipulative. It also prevents the needy person from receiving the benefit of support and affection from others. From a spiritual perspective, humility is the realization that God can use another person in someone's life just as easily as he can use me.

A caregiver with a healthy humility approaches needy people expecting to learn from them. If we think we know all there is to know about another person, we will not be able to care compassionately. We already have the person figured out so our interaction with him will only serve to substantiate our previous conclusions. Thus we treat the person merely as an intellectual challenge rather than as someone to be known and respected.

Humility allows those in our care to be themselves. We care for them because of their intrinsic worth, not because they meet our needs or society's needs. Humility demands that we give the same level of grace and understanding to each person in our care, regardless of the person's moral standards, socioeconomic level or physical and mental condition.

Humility enables us to be ourselves. If we have no pretensions, we are not humiliated when others see us as we truly are, for the image we project is our real self. We are free to rejoice with those who rejoice and weep with those who weep. We are able to become involved with those in our care and freely admit that we are as incurably human as they are.

Bev learned humility the hard way. Assigned to care for Martha, a young woman with AIDS, she resented the potential danger this woman posed to her own health. She spent as little time as possible with Martha and usually entered the room with a chip on her shoulder. Bev assumed that Martha had contracted HIV through intravenous drug use or sexual contact and inwardly felt she deserved what she got. Finally Martha apologized, "I'm so sorry I cause you all this trouble," and began to cry. Bev started to toss off a curt reply, when something stopped her. She apologized for her attitude and sat down with Martha.

As they talked, Martha shared her story. She had been married to a man who lived a double life. Bob was bisexual. He maintained the image of a loving husband and father while visiting gay bars on the sly. He contracted the AIDS virus from his homosexual contacts and brought it home to Martha, then left her for a male lover. Bob was also dying of AIDS. Bev learned to weep and rejoice with Martha, realizing she could easily have been in the same situation.

Commitment

Finally, if we are to offer compassionate presence, a degree of commitment is required. Commitment is a willingness on our part to share in the solitude, anxiety, suffering and grief of those in our care. When we offer compassionate presence to another, we have communicated a deep degree of commitment to that person by the nature of our involvement. We must be willing to continue that level of relationship as long as the person needs spiritual support.

That level of commitment is not easy, especially in chronic illness or long-term emotional problems. When Isabel, Lou's wife of forty-three years, died of cancer, members of his church rallied to provide food and frequent visits. They expected Lou to snap out of his grief in a few months, but he didn't. Instead, he turned inward, stopped attending church and rarely went out in public. He was angry at God for taking Isabel from him, and the anger spilled over toward anyone who visited. Most of the church visitors gradually stopped coming.

But Tom stuck with Lou. He visited several times a week, took Lou out to lunch, encouraged him to see his doctor and drove him to the appointments. They spent hours in silence together. At times Tom would simply bring paperwork to do at Lou's house. Occasionally Tom would offer to pray or share a passage of Scripture that had struck him personally, but most of the time he just stayed with Lou. Eventually Lou began to pour out his anger at God, his loneliness and his deep sense of loss. Tom listened and continued to offer his friendship. When Lou finally came out of his depression two years later, he credited Tom with saving his life.

To turn away from a person after beginning to intervene spiritually can be compared to a lifeguard's saying to a nonswimmer, "Come on into the water; it's safe—I'll hold you up," and then deciding to take his lunch break as the person takes his first tentative steps into the water. The emotional energy expended by a hurting person who begins to express his spiritual needs can be great. He may have had to overcome tremendous emotional barriers to open himself to another person on such a deep level. If we then refuse to continue our involvement, the person may hesitate to mention his spiritual needs again, just as the nonswimmer may develop a fear of the water after the lifeguard disappoints him. Commitment means dealing responsibly and compassionately for the long term.

Ultimately, commitment is the reflection of God's relationship with us. When we meet spiritual needs through compassionate presence, we often represent God to the other person. Our commitment or lack of commitment may determine a person's perception of God's love. For that reason, compassionate presence alone is insufficient for meeting spiritual needs. Our goal in spiritual care is to assist others in establishing and maintaining a dynamic personal relationship with God. Our aim is to direct their dependence toward God rather than ourselves. To do so, we need other resources beyond compassionate presence. Prayer, Scripture, corporate worship and participation in the full life of the church will place the focus on God as the true source of strength and healing.

Boundaries

Krista volunteered as a parish nurse in her congregation, but soon she found herself stretched for time and patience. Anna challenged her almost to the breaking point. Anna came regularly for blood-pressure checks. She usually unloaded a long list of seemingly trivial physical complaints as well as general fears and anxieties in regard to her family. Recently Anna had begun calling Krista every time she felt another problem coming on, usually just as Krista was trying to put her toddlers to bed. Krista felt torn between her children and Anna.

Finally, Krista told Anna that she could call her only once a week. They set a mutually convenient time. Krista limited the calls to ten minutes, explaining to Anna that this would be best for both of them. These boundaries helped wean Anna from overdependency—and helped keep Krista sane!

Commitment means keeping your promises and sticking with someone when the going gets tough (or tiresome), but it does not mean giving up all your personal boundaries. Even Jesus did not allow the needs of those around him to consume all his time and energy. Consider the following incident in his ministry:

> In the morning, while it was still very dark, he got up and went out to a deserted place, and there he prayed. And Simon and his companions hunted for him. When they found him, they said to him, "Everyone is searching for you." He answered, "Let us go on to the neighboring towns, so that I may proclaim the message there also; for that is what I came out to do." And he went throughout Galilee, proclaiming the message in their synagogues and casting out demons. (Mk 1:35-39)

We can draw some important principles from Jesus' example. First, he had a clear sense of priorities. His relationship with his Father came first. In that quiet time of prayer, he could draw strength and direction for his ministry. That gave him confidence and boldness to say no in order to say yes to what was most important. Anytime we begin to feel as if there is not enough time in the day to set aside a leisurely period for personal devotions, we can be pretty sure that we have taken on too many responsibilities.

Second, because Jesus gained his perspective from God, his actions were not based only on the demands of either his friends or those in need. Jesus did not heal everyone; he kept his overall purposes clear and could move on, even in the face of overwhelming need, to accomplish what his Father directed him to do. Any caring ministry can quickly become all-consuming. We will always see more needs than we are personally able to meet. Often those needs will make conflicting demands on our time. Sometimes Jesus handled the burden by delegating responsibility to others (Lk 10:1), sometimes he told people they were coming to him for the wrong things and sent them away (Jn 6:26), and numerous other times he simply left the crowds to go off alone to rest and pray (Mt 14:22-23; Lk 5:16; Jn 4:6).

Setting limits will almost always be difficult. You will receive unsolicited advice and criticism of your choices. But if our compassionate presence is to remain compassionate, we cannot exceed our personal resources in meeting the needs of others. If we do, we will eventually have nothing left to give.

6

Prayer

O*ur church's prayer ministry has become its greatest evangelism* program. No one planned it that way, but word spread throughout the community that our church prays. We receive calls from people with no formal church connections, asking for prayer. Total strangers come up to our members, asking if we will put their suffering family members on our prayer list. Often, when their prayers are answered as they hoped, those who made the requests attend worship services, giving God—and the prayers of the congregation—credit for their improved health.

To many people, prayer is a way of manipulating God into doing what they want. If their prayers aren't answered as they desire, they may become disillusioned and lose confidence in God. If prayer is answered according to their expectations, they feel good about God. However, true prayer is not a token in the heavenly vending machine. Prayer is an intimate conversation between a person and God. It is our response to God's initiative. Prayer recognizes our human limitations and our need for God. In many ways, it is a move out of the confusion of our situation toward a mature and steady hope. True prayer is a dialogue in which we open ourselves to God's will and direction, as well as communicating our requests, thoughts and feelings to God.

In a dynamic personal relationship with God, prayer serves as the vital lifeline in that relationship. Through prayer we receive perspective, power and the assurance of God's presence with us. The life and teachings of Jesus give us insight into the importance and meaning of prayer. He took time out of a busy schedule to be alone and pray (Mt 14:23). He shared his personal agony with God the Father in prayer (Mt 26:39). He interceded on behalf of those he loved (Jn 17). He also prayed for his enemies, as he taught his disciples to do (Lk 23:34). He taught about God's generosity in response to prayer (Mt 7:7-11), about the importance of coming to God humbly and simply (Mt 8:1-13), and about the power of praying in unity with others (Mt 18:19-20). In the Acts of the Apostles and the New Testament letters, we get a glimpse of the importance of prayer to early Christians. We see prayer as a dynamic link with a powerful and personal God. Prayer is vital to the spiritual life of Christians.

Illness Can Be a Barrier

Illness and crisis can create a barrier to personal prayer because the sick person's ability to sense God's presence may become clouded by the intensity of the problems. Consider Jerry Wells, a twenty-nine-year-old truck driver who was hospitalized with spinal injuries from an automobile accident. It was his second serious accident in six months. He had been active in church prior to this hospitalization, but when a nurse told him about the closed-circuit

TV chapel services on Sunday morning, he replied, "I don't think the Man Upstairs likes me anymore. We don't seem to be on speaking terms."

Jerry's reaction is not unusual. Mary Gowen, a twenty-five-year-old director of Christian education, became severely affected with colitis. She wrote in her diary, "My prayers don't seem to be getting through. I feel so selfish. I just keep dwelling on myself and praying for God to heal me. I can't seem to get beyond this point. I know God hears other people's prayers, but he doesn't seem to hear me."

Sarah Johnson had a similar response. A sixty-nine-year-old grandmother who had always had a deep faith, she confessed to a parish nurse, "God seems so far away right now. I don't understand it, but I can't seem to pray anymore."

Illness and suffering often disrupt a person's ability to pray. The normal stages of grief affect a person's relationship with God, as well as relationships with other people. Jerry Wells may feel God does not hear, does not care or does not know about his concerns. He may blame God for his accident and be angry toward God—and then feel guilt over his anger. He may try to bargain with God and then give up in despair. He may be so overwhelmed by his present situation that he thinks no one, including God, can help him. In any case, Jerry, Mary and Sarah feel they are not getting through to God.

Figure 3 provides a picture of these dynamics. The dotted lines indicate the reality of the relationships. The woman in the wheelchair has a relationship with God, but her illness hangs like a cloud, making God seem distant and unconcerned. However, she can see the nurse's presence and sense her compassion. She communicates easily with her. She also senses that the nurse has a strong faith relationship with God. She knows that God listens to this nurse. When the nurse prays for her, she feels that God hears her concerns. The nurse's praying aloud with Sarah assures Sarah that the prayers will be heard.

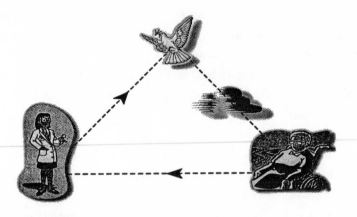

Figure 3. Why pray?

A Sense of Isolation

Most seriously ill people experience an overwhelming sense of isolation at some point. Whether or not the person has a strong support system, he or she often feels alone and cut off from human relationships. Maria, a thirty-three-year-old woman with a brain tumor, described her sense of isolation: "It is difficult to express the deep inner cravings of my heart during these last few months. I longed night and day for someone to reach out to me with an understanding hand and heart. It was as if I had a huge, gaping wound that could not be treated. The pain, the fear, the irritability, the turmoil pressed upon me daily. It seemed as though no one was near me, no one cared. I thought I would collapse for want of understanding. I felt that I must be the only person to have ever experienced such a need." The fact that warm, loving friends and family surround the person does not always cut through that sense of isolation.

When people cannot perceive the love and concern of other people, whom they can see, their ability to sense God's presence and concern is even further impaired. When that illness forces them into dependency upon others, the emotional struggle surrounding loss of control and independence may further complicate their ability to trust in God.

Often persons who have had a strong faith will undergo the most distressing difficulties in their ability to trust God and to pray. Prior to her brain tumor, Maria was a missionary with a vibrant faith, yet she concluded, "I needed someone to say in words the things I was unable to say to God." She felt comforted because others were praying for her, but she also felt guilty that she suddenly seemed estranged from God. She desperately wanted to trust God, but at the same time, she felt angry and betrayed by him. All of the hurts and perceived failures of her missionary career came crashing down on her, sending her into a spiral of fear and depression. Her friend Ginny listened quietly as Maria shared her feelings, then offered to pray with her. In her prayer Ginny told God exactly what Maria had told her, asking him to give Maria strength, peace and healing. As Ginny prayed, Maria began to feel hopeful.

Our prayers for others are important not only for the comfort they may receive but because God hears our prayers and answers. We have a responsibility to pray *for* those who are suffering. However, praying *with* them has additional advantages beyond the psychological ones. Jesus instructed the disciples, "If two of you agree on earth about anything you ask, it will be done for you by my Father in heaven" (Mt 18:19). Praying together is important to God.

Praying together is also important to the sick person. When we say, "I'll pray for you," without finding out what the person wants us to pray *for*, we may be of some comfort, but we offer only minimal support. The person never knows what we will pray or has the assurance that we really *did* pray.

When Ginny prayed aloud for Maria, Maria knew that someone had truly heard her concerns and understood her needs. Ginny facilitated Maria's relationship to God as she became a temporary channel of God's grace. She also broke through the interpersonal isolation that Maria felt as she joined her in bearing her burden before the Lord.

Intimacy Without Exposure

Shared prayer has some unique interpersonal side effects; it can be one of the deepest forms of human communication. Hospital chaplain Daniel DeArment claims that shared prayer allows "intimacy without exposure."[1] When we pray with a patient, expressing to God what the patient has told us verbally and nonverbally, we break through the person's isolation without directly discussing what we have observed that was not verbalized. For instance, a person may deny he is fearful of surgery, but his affect betrays him. To confront that person directly by saying, "You *are* afraid; I can tell," would probably send his defenses up further. But to pray with him, "Lord, this is a scary situation—comfort John tonight," might free him to talk about the fear he is experiencing.

The question of meaning, especially finding meaning in an illness, can be dealt with more deeply in shared prayer than in casual conversation. A relationship with God can supply meaning when human resources cannot satisfactorily explain the suffering. In praying with patients we do more than support them; we join them in their quest for meaning and purpose by going with them to the Source.

When a crisis has distorted a person's view of God, we may be able to demonstrate a healthy picture of God through shared prayer. For instance, someone we are caring for may feel that God is far away and does not hear. As we address God personally and confidently, the suffering person's perception of God's love and concern may be renewed.

The work of the Holy Spirit through us and within us cannot be explained scientifically, but it is a reality. Romans 8:26 states, "Likewise the Spirit helps us in our weakness; for we do not know how to pray as we ought, but that very Spirit intercedes with sighs too deep for words." The observable interpersonal dynamics—the sense of intimacy and unity—which result from shared prayer are not a psychological gimmick. They demonstrate the power of a personal God at work in his creatures.

When to Pray

Prayer must be used in the context of compassionate presence, in a relationship in which adequate communication has taken place. When a person has expressed pain, fear, anxiety, stress, helplessness or joy (either verbally or nonverbally) to the extent that we can identify what the person is feeling, then we can pray appropriately. If you do not have a fairly clear understanding of what is bothering the other person, you are not yet ready to pray. Praying prematurely with someone is likely to cut off further in-depth communication.

On the other hand, be careful to avoid using prayer as a way to end a conversation or visit. Prayer often triggers deep feelings within a person. The verbal interaction after shared prayer may be more significant than the conversation beforehand. DeArment states, "A further test of dynamic and thoroughly legitimate use of prayer at the bedside is your willingness to stay and respond to the feelings and words of the patients which the prayer has touched."[2]

In situations where anxiety is high, be alert for spiritual needs. Times of waiting and uncertainty provide opportunities to pray with others. Prayer can be especially helpful preoperatively, before major tests, after admission to an unfamiliar environment or when potentially frightening equipment is applied (such as ventilators, electrodes or monitors).

Early in my nursing career, Rosella Valenti taught me the value of prayer in a time of high anxiety, hers and mine. Recently reassigned to the intensive care unit, I still felt unsure of my competence when Rosella was admitted after a major heart attack. Rosella belonged to my church, but I did not know her well. She seemed relieved to see me there and asked me to pray for her, which I did. The head nurse was not pleased. She sternly warned me to keep my religious practices out of her unit. The next morning, however, Rosella seemed delirious, complaining loudly about the "green men" who had violated her privacy and treated her roughly. She seemed to think she was on a spaceship. She continually cried out, "Oh God, help me!"

Then I caught a glimpse of a surgical team making rounds in their green scrub suits and considered how Rosella must feel in her cubicle, attached to monitors that beeped and an IV catheter dripping a strange solution into her veins. Of course those men must have looked like aliens from outer space! I went to the head nurse and told her that I honestly thought I should pray with Rosella, explaining that it might calm her. Then I gently laid my hand on Rosella's arm, explained where she was and what was happening, and prayed for her. She relaxed, smiled and said, "I really did know those men were doctors, I was just so scared—but I know the Lord is here too." She never "hallucinated" again—and I had blanket permission to pray for patients after that.

A basic guideline to determine whether prayer is appropriate in a given situation might be to ask yourself, "Whose need am I meeting—my own or the other person's?" If your own need compels you to pray, then you would do better to pray privately, rather than to use the suffering person to meet your need. If I had indiscriminately prayed aloud with every patient in the ICU, the head nurse would have been entirely justified in reprimanding me. However, because I assessed her need for prayer first, my intervention with Rosella became clearly appropriate.

Rarely will a person turn down your offer to pray. I can only think of two occasions when this happened in my own experience. Both incidents occurred when I was visiting as a hospital chaplain, never when I was caring for someone as a nurse. One situation was an older woman, who told me, "No, my own pastor is coming this afternoon." The other was a high-powered businessman, who seemed to need to feel in control. He said, "I'll be fine, I don't need any help from the Man Upstairs." When this happens, respect the person's refusal and simply continue with your conversation. Communicate acceptance of the person, even if he or she does not accept your offer. Be sure you don't just turn on your heel and leave at that point.

How to Pray

When we pray with a person, we express to God what that person would pray if able. The most helpful prayer is usually a short, simple statement to God of the person's hopes, fears and needs, and a recognition of God's ability to meet the person in his or her situation.

For example, Rose Wade was admitted to the emergency department with a gunshot wound of the nose and mouth inflicted by her husband during an argument. Her condition was stable. She was alert, but she could not talk because of the pain and swelling of her tongue. She appeared frightened and uncomfortable. After orienting her to her surroundings, a nurse brought her a pencil and paper and asked her to write down any questions or needs. Rose wrote, "Where are my babies? What did they do with my husband? How long do I have to stay here?" The nurse promised to try to find the answers to Rose's questions and went out to the desk to make the necessary phone calls.

The children were located at a neighbor's house. The nurse then called the neighbor from Rose's bedside phone to reassure Rose that they were fine. Her husband was in jail. Rose's physician could give no estimate of the length of her stay. It would depend on her progress. After receiving the information she requested, Rose seemed less distressed but still quite anxious. She wrote, "I love my husband. It was an *accident*. I don't want them to lock him up!" Then she lay back with a hopeless look. The nurse asked, "Rose, would you like me to pray with you?" Rose looked relieved and nodded.

The nurse prayed, "Father, thank you that you know what's going on in all this confusion. Thank you that Rose's babies are being well cared for. We pray that you will be with her husband in jail and ask that he will be treated fairly. Give him peace, Lord. Help him to know that Rose loves him and you love him. Give strength and healing to Rose now, so she can go home soon. She's frightened now, Lord; please comfort her. In Jesus' name. Amen."

In the prayer, the nurse mentioned problems that Rose expressed: her babies, her husband and her length of stay. The nurse, sensitive to Rose's nonverbal communication, also prayed that her husband would know Rose loved him. At that point in the prayer, Rose began to weep, indicating that a deep feeling had been touched. The nurse also recognized Rose's fear in the prayer, although they had not discussed it directly. The nurse prayed what Rose would have prayed had she been able.

If we are to pray as the other person would pray, we need to consider the religious background of the person, including the types of prayers which have been meaningful to that person in the past. Most people appreciate the simple, informal expression of their needs to God, but many have been accustomed to formal, written prayers. Some people may even feel that spontaneous prayers are disrespectful to God and may prefer a selection from a prayer book. The Lord's Prayer usually touches a deep chord in most Christians—both Protestants and Roman Catholics. Even demented and semicomatose people will often be able to pray the Lord's Prayer with you, though they are unable to respond to other verbal stimuli.

When the other person comes from a non-Christian background, you can still offer to pray to God. That offer will usually be graciously accepted. However, if the person insists on praying to another god, you can simply say, "I can't do that, but I will try to find someone else who can help you." Most hospital chaplains' departments will be able to find appropriate spiritual leaders from various faith traditions. Even Jesus allowed people to make their own choices, giving them the freedom to turn away from him (Mt 19:22).

At other times, you may feel unable to pray what a person would like you to pray. For example, Alma Stanton lay in bed moaning and grasping the stump where her leg had been amputated. As Megan Hill passed her doorway, Alma called out, "Nurse, nurse, please pray for me."

Megan entered the room and sat down. "What do you want me to pray for?"

"Pray that my leg would grow back," Alma replied. What could Megan say to Mrs. Stanton? If she prayed for Alma as requested, she would reinforce Alma's unrealistic expectations. Prayer would be reduced to magic. Alma might see God as a genie who grants wishes. If Alma's leg did not grow back, she might be convinced that God had failed her and did not really care about her.

Megan could say, "Alma, I can't do that. Both you and I know that your leg will not grow back." Although this approach is reality-based, it would be treating Alma in a condescending manner. She might stop communicating her needs altogether. Alma needed love and support from Megan and from God, not criticism.

A more constructive response would be, "It must really hurt to lose a leg." Megan would then be giving Alma an opening to talk about the loss she was experiencing, offering an empathetic ear. After Alma had had the opportunity to express her concerns related to the loss of her leg, Megan would be able to pray more specifically for Alma's needs. How, then, could Megan turn Alma's magical expectations into an appropriate and compassionate prayer?

In talking with Alma, Megan found she was afraid of becoming dependent on her children or being forced to go to a nursing home. Her progress in physical therapy had been slow. She lived alone and was not sure she would be able to care for herself. She was also experiencing phantom pains in her amputated leg, which made her wonder if she was losing her mind. After talking with Alma a few minutes, Megan asked, "Why don't we pray about the things we've been talking about?" Alma agreed. Megan prayed, "Heavenly Father, thank you that you know Alma and love her very much. Thank you, too, that you know her needs. Father, you know how frightened she is right now. Her life seems to be changing so much all at once, and there are so many unknowns. Father, give her courage and strength. Help her in physical therapy, and give her confidence as she learns to walk with the artificial leg.

Lord, we know that you are in control of Alma's future, and you will provide for her as she leaves the hospital. Give her your peace right now. Ease her pain, and let her get some good rest tonight. Thank you for being with her. In Jesus' name. Amen."

Megan's prayer communicated that God loved Alma, knew her needs and was present with her. It was specifically related to the needs Alma expressed, but it did not raise unrealistic expectations.

Can We Ever Pray for Healing?

Prayer is not magic. Prayer is communication in a personal relationship with God. We cannot manipulate God by demanding unrealistic answers. At what point does it become inappropriate to ask God for results? How specific can we be with our responses? Can we ever pray for healing? If so, when?

Perhaps the most helpful guidelines on how to pray come from a clear understanding of the nature of God's relationship with us. Communication with our heavenly Father is not unlike talking with our earthly parents. Because we know our parents well, we soon learn to anticipate which requests will be granted and which will not. In a healthy parent-child relationship, the child also knows his parents love him, even if they do not allow him to do or have everything he wants. A child comes to his parents for other reasons besides making requests. He shares his activities and his dreams. He communicates love and appreciation. He learns to say thank you.

Prayer involves the same type of interaction as child-parent communication. God-as-heavenly-Father is a much more mature view of God than God-as-genie. When we approach God as our Father in our prayers, we are sharing a mature concept of God with those with whom we are praying.

The Bible presents God as a loving Father who gives "good

things to those who ask him" (Mt 7:11). Included in those good things is healing. Healing in a biblical sense, however, is more inclusive than mere physical healing. Health and salvation are closely related in Scripture. The Hebrew word for *salvation* may also be translated "saving health." God is concerned about the whole person. We are told in the Scriptures to pray for healing (for example, Jas 5:13-15). Physical healing may result from our prayers of faith (Lk 8:48; 18:42), but not necessarily (2 Cor 12:8-9; 1 Tim 5:23; 2 Tim 4:20). God's central concern is that each person live in vital relationship to him.

When we pray with others, we bring comfort and encouragement through supporting the person's relationship with God. We can also facilitate that relationship by providing assistance with personal devotions or arranging a visit from a pastor when desired. Prayer is a vital link with God. We help suffering people experience God's meaning and purpose, his love and his forgiveness as we pray aloud with them.

Healing services in churches provide another context for healing prayer. Many churches invite people to come forward for prayer and to be anointed with oil. Other churches provide opportunities for prayer in small groups, or for the pastor or elders to visit those who are sick or suffering and pray for them. Whether in a formal church service or in one-to-one conversation, prayer is the language of family relationship and our expression of belonging to the family of God.

7

The Bible

My friend Phyllis suffered severe back pain for years, but suddenly her situation moved from chronic to acute when she began to lose feeling and function in her legs. When she was hospitalized for some painful procedures, I agreed to stay with her for a couple of days. While sitting with Phyllis after the procedure, I worked on a Bible study on Psalm 66 that I was preparing for a retreat. Suddenly, several verses jumped out at me:

> For you, O God, have tested us; you have tried us as silver is tried. You brought us into the net; you laid burdens on our backs; you let people ride over our heads; we went through fire and through water; yet you have brought us out to a spacious place. (Ps 66:10-12)

These verses seemed to be what Phyllis had been experiencing in her own recent struggle. She had been working toward a major job change when her health problems overwhelmed her. The burdens on her back were literal, as well as figurative. The physical pain had become unbearable. Every time she began to feel a little better, her physicians suggested another test or therapy, each more painful than the previous ones. Her condition did not improve, yet she faced the heavy demands of her present job while the increasing responsibilities for her future direction impinged upon her. She felt that she was letting everyone down.

"Phyllis, listen to this—it sounds like a message just for you!" I exclaimed. Phyllis listened, still groggy from the anesthetic, concentrating as well as she could. The part about the "spacious place" caught her attention. Later, she asked me to read it again, and she clung to those verses as a promise. She shared them with her colleagues when she finally returned to work, included them in her letters to others and repeated them often. God spoke through his Word and gave her hope.

Using Scripture with persons who are ill or facing crisis may provide hope, strength and peace, but it can also deeply wound or disillusion. When sharing Scripture, you must choose passages carefully and share them appropriately. In the story of Job and his suffering, Job's "comforters" are a good example of sharing Scripture inappropriately.

What did these "comforters" do wrong? First, they came in with the assumption that anyone who suffered must deserve the affliction. Second, they never asked Job how he felt, or supported what resources he had left; they simply condemned him. The Bible can too easily be used as a club. I have even heard people quoting Job's friends to sick people, assuming that since those words are in the Bible, they must be the word of God for those who suffer.

How Not to Use the Bible

Peggy felt the full blows of this approach. She was hospitalized for a severe septicemia complicated by congestive heart failure and gross obesity, and none of the medical treatments seemed to be working. Peggy grew increasingly discouraged as she lay listlessly in her hospital bed. Then one of the nurses popped into her room carrying a Bible. "I want to read you something, Peggy," she began, turning to John 14:13-14. "'I will do whatever you ask in my name, so that the Father may be glorified in the Son. If in my name you ask me for anything, I will do it.'" Then she continued, "Do you know why you aren't getting any better? You don't have enough faith! If you had faith, God would heal you."

Peggy did not respond. She felt as if she had been stabbed in the back. She walked closely with the Lord, but right now she just couldn't work up any more faith, and she knew in her head that the nurse's assumption simply was not true. It still hurt to hear those words, though.

Finally the nurse chirped, "Do you know how many Christian nurses there are in this hospital?"

Peggy's latent sense of humor rallied as she responded, "Probably one less than you think!"

Just because words are in the Bible does not mean they are equally appropriate for every situation. The Bible contains stories, arguments, poems, proverbs, laws, personal correspondence and rich imagery. Although it is completely inspired by God, it is also a very human book, written in a historical and social context. Particular sections are directed toward specific situations and cultural settings. It is a book full of human emotions and failings, as well as a record of the victory of God in and through his people. While the Holy Spirit meets us in its pages and changes us, the Bible is not a magic book that can be used for incantations or healing formulas—although people through the centuries have tried to do so.

Jerry Caldwell, a senior seminarian, found himself in deep trouble one morning when visiting a member of the church where he was assigned. A severe diabetic, Ethel was recuperating from a below-the-knee amputation. Jerry offered to read a passage of Scripture to Ethel, indiscriminately choosing Psalm 121. As he read verse 3, he choked on his own words, "He will not let your foot be moved." Ethel sat up indignantly, remarking, "Well, he certainly didn't keep his promise this time, did he?"

A final caution in choosing Bible verses is to avoid using your favorite verses as pat answers. Romans 8:28 is probably the most abused passage in this regard: "We know that all things work together for good for those who love God, who are called according to his purpose." As Dan replied after hearing this verse quoted too many times, "I know God is good and he loves me, but right now I'm scared and hurting, and I just want someone to listen."

Using the Bible Appropriately

Dan gives us the first principle for using the Bible appropriately. Whenever you read or quote Scripture to someone who is suffering, be sure to *listen carefully first.* Scripture should always be used in conjunction with compassionate presence. What is the person thinking and feeling? How does the person view God? How has the illness or disability affected the person's relationship with God?

For example, Dorothy felt that God had abandoned her in her long battle with ovarian cancer. She had been a faithful church member all her life and had never doubted God until now. Her wavering trust in God deeply disturbed her. When her pastor, Bill Moser, visited, he listened to Dorothy's concerns without comment. Finally, Bill looked her in the eye and said, "Even David felt that way sometimes, Dorothy—listen to Psalm 13." Then he read, "How long, O LORD? Will you forget me forever? How long will you hide your face from me? How long must I bear pain in my soul, and have sorrow in my heart all day long?" (Ps 13:1-2).

Passages that enable a person to identify with a biblical character may bring comfort to those who feel guilty about not accepting their condition or who may be angry with God or with other people. Once you have listened carefully to what a person is really thinking and feeling, you will be able to choose passages that will encourage and support the person. You will also need to be familiar with a wide variety of Scripture to choose appropriate passages.

The passages in figure 4 have proved especially helpful to people in distress. Read through these references and think about situations in which each might be appropriate to share with someone. You may also want to discuss them with several other people to hear their insights. Begin keeping a log using the verses in figure 4; then continue by adding your own favorites to the list.

Part of listening carefully includes *considering the appropriate timing* when sharing Scripture. Romans 8:28 may be a helpful passage to suggest to someone who has begun to express a glimmer of hope and merely needs reinforcement for what God is already teaching. But when someone is feeling angry at God, it may intensify the pain. The suffering person may be feeling, "Sure, everything is working out for good in everyone else's life, but not for me!" This person may actually be comforted by the psalms of lament, such as Psalm 13, where the psalmist complains, "How long, O LORD?" or Psalm 88, with its similar theme.

Even the angry portions that we cringe to read can be helpful to someone who is in the anger stage of grief. Reading a passage such as Psalm 94 or Psalm 139:19-22 may be an emotional cathar-

	Guilt	Loneliness	Abandonment	Suffering	Fear of unknown	Fear of death	Chronic illness	Notes
Deut 7:6-9								
Neh 9:17								
Ps 4								
Ps 13								
Ps 16								
Ps 23								
Ps 32								
Ps 51								
Ps 61								
Ps 88								
Ps 116								
Ps 139								
Is 30:15,18								
Is 61:1-3								
Mt 11:28-30								
Jn 11:25-26								
Jn 14:1-7								
Rom 8:1-4								
Rom 8:26-28								
Rom 8:38-39								
Phil 4:4-7								
Heb 4:15-16								
Heb 13:5-6								
1 Jn 1:8-9								

Figure 4. Helpful Bible passages

sis for those who are feeling guilty about their anger. Many suffering people go through an intense time of being angry at God, so it is comforting to know that even people in the Bible got angry and discouraged.

For instance, Frank Washington had been shuffled around the health care system until his physical condition seriously deteriorated. No one seemed to know what to do, and each attempt at diagnosis and treatment simply made his condition worse. He felt angry at God and just about everyone else, yet embarrassed to express that anger. It scared him, and he feared God might actually reject him if he admitted his real feelings. However, his friend Lamont sensed how he felt. He had been there several years before. "Frank, there's a psalm I want to read to you," Lamont began tentatively. "It's long, but bear with me. I think you'll relate." As Lamont began reading portions of Psalm 69, Frank wept. When he got to verse 29, Frank began to cheer up. By the time they reached the end, Frank was praising God.

Peace and comfort are not the only ways to measure the effectiveness of your spiritual care, though. Hebrews tells us, "Indeed, the word of God is living and active, sharper than any two-edged sword, piercing until it divides soul from spirit, joints from marrow; it is able to judge the thoughts and intentions of the heart" (Heb 4:12). While we should not use the Bible to condemn or judge people, sometimes the Holy Spirit will use it to convict people of sin. It may spur them to anger or drive them to deep introspection. Don't be disturbed if someone responds negatively to a particular passage. However, be very careful that any offense comes from the Word itself and not from your insensitivity to the person's real needs.

Choosing the right Bible translation may also influence the effectiveness of the Scripture you read. Most people will appreciate hearing an understandable modern version. However, some may consider the King James Version the only acceptable translation. It is best to ask if those you are caring for have a preference. You may even want to use the other person's Bible. Once, in my enthusiasm for a particular new translation, I read to a patient from it without thinking. She looked horrified when she saw the cover and exclaimed, "Get out of here with that—don't you know that Bible is of the devil? They took the blood out!" I went home, checked to make sure *the blood* was still there (it was) and considered it a lesson learned the hard way.

An attractive way to share Scripture is using colorful presentations on cards or bookmarks that are carefully chosen for this particular person. You can make them yourself or get them in Christian bookstores or from Bible societies. You might also want to keep some small, easy-to-hold and large-print Scripture booklets handy to give to people in your care. Many are now available in topical collections with lovely illustrations. You can also find booklets of Psalms, the Gospel of John, the book of Job and other portions of Scripture that are particularly encouraging to those who are suffering. Also remember that people who do not speak English as their primary language will appreciate receiving Bibles or other Christian literature in their first language.

Learning from Those Who Suffer

Spiritual growth should be a shared experience. Providing spiritual care does not mean that we are always in the position of teachers. Let those in your care teach you from their own understanding of Scripture. Although many suffering people have enriched my life with their insights into Scripture, one particular woman stands out. Anna Morris was a frequent patient on the surgical unit where I worked as a nurse. Each time she came back, her cancer had progressed further, which made me dread each readmission. However, while her body deteriorated, her spirit soared, and she joyfully shared her walk with the Lord. She would pray for other patients on the unit—and pray for the nurses. Every morning she would greet me with a cheerful, "Here's your verse for today!" The verse was always amazingly appropriate and became a great source of encouragement throughout the day. Whenever I stopped into her room, she would ask how my day was going and briefly discuss why she saw that particular verse as significant for me.

Asking others about their favorite Bible passages or inquiring about which verses seem particularly helpful at this time will give opportunity for them to share with you what God is teaching them. It also provides an opening for them to reminisce about God's faithfulness over a lifetime. Listening to them may be as encouraging to you as it is to the ones you are trying to serve.

Other Written Resources

Popular Christian literature that deals with illness, suffering and death abounds today. Much of this material can support, encourage and guide readers. When you consider recommending books to those in your care, keep in mind some important principles.

First, *keep it short*. People in crisis, or those who are distracted by pain or disabilities, will have limited attention spans. Even people who are ordinarily heavy readers may not be able to read more than a few pages at a time. Large print and short chapters will be welcome. A small, lightweight book will be easier to hold for someone reading in bed. Devotional books designed for times of illness or crisis may be especially appreciated. Granger Westberg's little classic, *Good Grief: A Constructive Approach to the Problem of Loss*

(Minneapolis: Fortress, 1986), is an excellent example. It is sixty-four pages long and available in large print.

Second, the book should be *practical.* Instructions that are clear, concise and to the point will be extremely helpful. For instance, if a family is considering placing an aging parent in an extended-care facility, they might greatly appreciate a book that lists important factors to consider. Numerous resources with checklists or step-by-step instructions are constantly being produced.

Third, be sure that the information is *accurate and up-to-date.* Health care systems and medical regimens change rapidly today, so even a fairly recent book may be out-of-date. If you do not feel qualified to evaluate a book for accuracy, ask a nurse or physician with expertise in the field you are concerned about to recommend an appropriate resource.

Fourth, look for books that are *personal.* Don't recommend a book that you have not read yourself. You should be able to provide a personal recommendation—either because it helped you through difficult times in your own life or because you specifically chose the book to meet the needs of the recipient. It should also be personal in the sense that the author speaks from firsthand experience as a survivor or caregiver.

Books that share rather than preach will be most encouraging. For instance, books by Joni Eareckson Tada (who was paralyzed in a diving accident), Dave Dravecki (who lost an arm to cancer) and Walter Wangerin (who writes as a caring pastor) teach by telling compelling stories that deal directly with the harsh realities of suffering, yet point to God's love and faithfulness.

Finally, always *follow up* when you offer a book to someone. Ask if your friend would like to discuss certain chapters or has questions about anything. If poor eyesight or other physical disabilities limit the person's ability to read, you could offer to read portions aloud.

Hearing the Word

Many people today simply don't read, even when they are healthy. Illness may make reading difficult. Video- and audiotapes provide a wealth of resources in such times. Christian music, Scripture and whole books are available in both formats. Sometimes when people are in crisis the words of Scripture will communicate more clearly through hymns and praise songs than they will through reading.

When my friend Phyllis was ill, she spent hours playing a series of tapes produced by Moody Video that showed beautiful scenery accompanied by Scripture readings and hymns. She also began recalling hymns from her childhood that spoke to her of God's faithfulness, and she deeply appreciated hearing someone play them on the piano.

Many times when words don't comfort, the gentle strains of a familiar hymn will connect. It is not at all unusual for someone who appears to be semiconscious to sing along, remembering the words of hymns that they have known for many years.

God communicates to us through his Word. We read it in the Scriptures and hear it when the Bible is read, but other Christian literature and multimedia presentations also attest to that Word. When people are unable to take it in for themselves, our spiritual care needs to focus on helping them hear the Word of God and find comfort in his love and faithfulness.

8

The Power
of Touch

Soon after his arrival, the new pastor instituted a time in the worship services when the congregation was supposed to greet one another with a warm handshake or a hug. Some of the old-timers gathered around after church complaining about this practice, but eighty-seven-year-old Doris Martin declared, "Well, I *like* it! I never miss church, because it is the only time anyone touches me anymore. Besides, didn't Paul tell the church in Rome to greet one another with a holy kiss?" Doris's husband had died four years earlier. She lived alone, remaining healthy and self-sufficient, but she missed human touch.

Jesus used touch throughout his ministry. A leper approached him, saying, "Lord, if you choose, you can make me clean." Jesus stretched out his hand and touched him, saying, "I do choose. Be made clean!" His leprosy was cleansed on the spot (Mt 8:2-3). He touched the hand of Peter's sick mother-in-law, and she was healed (Mt 8:15). A woman with chronic vaginal bleeding touched the fringe of his cloak and was healed (Mt 9:22). He touched the eyes of two blind men, and their eyes were opened (Mt 9:29). Matthew continues to explain, "After the people of that place recognized him, they sent word throughout the region and brought all who were sick to him, and begged him that they might touch even the fringe of his cloak; and all who touched it were healed" (Mt 14:35-36).

Another woman came to Jesus with "a spirit that had crippled her for eighteen years. She was bent over and was quite unable to stand up straight. When Jesus saw her, he called her over and said, 'Woman, you are set free from your ailment.' When he laid his hands on her, immediately she stood up straight and began praising God" (Lk 13:11-13).

In the context of these healings, Jesus told his disciples, "Very truly, I tell you, the one who believes in me will also do the works that I do and, in fact, will do greater works than these, because I am going to the Father" (Jn 14:12). However, he did not use touch only for healing. When the disciples were overcome by fear, "Jesus came and touched them, saying, 'Get up and do not be afraid'" (Mt 17:7). Touch communicates tenderness, affection, strength and acceptance. The psalmist cried out, "Do not be far from me, for trouble is near and there is no one to help" (Ps 22:11). Touch lets a suffering person know that someone is near.

When touch is absent, a person may feel alone and abandoned. The psalmist complained, "You have caused my companions to shun me; you have made me a thing of horror to them. I am shut in so that I cannot escape; my eye grows dim through sorrow. Every day I call on you, O LORD; I spread out my hands to you" (Ps 88:8-9). When we are afraid or in pain, the natural response is to reach out and touch another person for support. And the psalmist reminds himself, "For he will command his angels concerning you to guard you in all your ways. On their hands they will bear you up, so that you will not dash your foot against a stone" (Ps 91:11-12). We want to be touched by other people, by God and, when we are desperate, by angels.

Touch also keeps us in contact with reality. When Jesus returned from the dead and appeared to the disciples, he told them, "Look at my hands and my feet; see that it is I myself. Touch me and see; for a ghost does not have flesh and bones as you see that I have" (Lk 24:39). In the same way, touch can often help a person who is afraid or disoriented to relax and feel comfortable in strange surroundings.

The Dynamics of Touch

Everybody needs physical touch. "During the nineteenth century," writes anthropologist Ashley Montagu, "more than half the infants in their first year regularly died from a disease called *marasmus*, a Greek word meaning 'wasting away.'" This disease was characterized by a gradual loss of muscle and strength for no apparent reason. Montagu goes on to say that as late as the 1920s the death rate for infants under one year of age in various foundling institutions in the United States was nearly 100 percent. The cause of marasmus was not identified until after World War II, when research showed it was due to a lack of nurture. Both physically and emotionally, a child needs to be carried, caressed and cuddled.[1]

Nursing has traditionally incorporated touch into routine care: assisting a patient with bathing, offering back rubs during evening care, supporting an unstable person while walking, providing skin care, positioning a patient in bed and giving an occasional gentle, caring touch. Many of these practices are getting lost in the current high-tech health care environment or being relegated to assistive personnel.

Touch communicates caring and intimacy. A gentle hand on the arm or shoulder, a pat on the back or holding a hand will usually provide strength and encouragement to another person. Healthy friendships also involve touch that is nurturing and comforting without being erotic. The importance of touch for healthy emotional development is now commonly understood. It communicates involvement, concern, responsibility, tenderness and awareness of the needs and vulnerabilities of the other. We do not lose that need for touch as adults; in fact, it is those adults who are feeling alone and lacking intimacy who seem to be most at risk for an emotionally dependent relationship.

Pastor Michael Phillips explains, "When someone is hurting, affection is more than a warm fuzzy or a mild turn-on. Intimacy is the bonding of comfort, the balm of closeness, the first and greatest expression of understanding."[2] Sadly, touch is often misinterpreted in our culture. People who have been sexually abused may shrink from physical touch. Others may assume it communicates more than intended, responding sexually. However, while recognizing the dangers involved in expressing affection, Phillips insists that "intimacy is not an enemy" and sets some guidelines. He avoids showing affection when his own emotions are unstable, when the other person turns away and when it does not express true relationship. However, he finds it appropriate in the face of loss, in times of discouragement and when a person is feeling rejected.[3]

Counselor Lori Rentzel offers some suggestions (while warning that there is no quick fix) for times when sexual attraction does become a problem and affection becomes manipulative. First, we need to be honest with ourselves and God about the problem, acknowledging the inappropriate aspects of the relationship. Next, it is important to be honest about the problem with another person who can counsel and pray with us. Then we must gradually begin separating from the relationship.[4]

Guidelines for Appropriate Touch

Although touch is essential for healthy relationships, each person perceives touch differently. The toucher's intentions may be misinterpreted—either positively or negatively. Some basic guidelines will keep touch appropriate and helpful.

☐ Ask permission before touching. "May we hold hands while we pray?" "May I give you a hug?" A gentle touch on the arm or shoulder might be okay without asking permission, but if the person pulls back or stiffens, consider that a no! Remember that the other person may sense an imbalance of power and fear rejection on saying no, so be alert for body language.

☐ Consider the cultural background of the other person before touching. Asians are generally more reserved and may be offended by touch from a stranger. A Chinese friend once confessed to me that she felt terrified when her Western friends greeted her with a hug. Latinos are usually open and demonstrative. However, stereotypes don't always fit, so ask.

☐ Be careful where you touch. The breasts, genitals, buttocks and thighs are off-limits. The arms, shoulders or back are usually safe places to touch. Avoid any suggestion of sexual touch. Long, tight frontal hugs, fondling or caressing are always inappropriate in a helping relationship. Even light touch or quick hugs between the sexes can be interpreted as flirting. If you or the other person feel uncomfortable with the touch, avoid it.

☐ For the most part, avoid touching when you are alone with a person, especially in a counseling situation. While it would be quite appropriate to hold the hand of a terminally ill person if you were alone at the bedside or to give a quick hug of greeting to a shut-in, beware of prolonged or frequent touching in situations where no one else is around.

☐ When you are counseling with someone, it is wise to leave the door ajar so that caring touch will not be misinterpreted. If you suspect that the other person (either male or female) may be growing overly dependent or attached to you, avoid touching in private situations.

☐ Be careful not to make the person feel cornered or forced to accept your affection.

☐ Tickling or playful aggression are usually inappropriate.

Sexual abuse is a serious problem in our society. Sometimes touch that begins as innocent, caring gestures can escalate into sexual behavior. When the person initiating the touch is in a position of power, such as a nurse, pastor or other caregiver, the other person may be afraid to object or stop it. The person who feels violated may then feel responsible for causing the problem; shame and long-term emotional distress can follow. People who have been touch-deprived may misinterpret touch or respond sexually when the one touching simply intended to communicate compassion.

Abuses of Touch

Sexual misconduct is not the only abuse of touch. Many new "touch therapies" are appearing on the health care scene and are being offered as "alternative" or "complementary" therapies. Both health care professionals and the general public are being misled by the media and by respected health care institutions.

For example, Mary Palumbo, in the late stages of ovarian cancer, deeply appreciated the support and practical assistance of her hospice nurse, Sue Mason. Sue had worked with Mary until her pain was under good control, and she enabled Mary and her family to talk about her impending death together. However, Sue sensed a restlessness in Mary that nothing seemed to touch.

The hospice had recently provided an inservice education program on Therapeutic Touch, and Sue decided to try the technique on Mary. Sue explained the procedure to Mary as a form of what the church has always practiced as the "laying on of hands." Mary felt uncomfortable with the idea, but consented.

First Sue "centered" herself by sitting quietly and practicing some meditative techniques, including deep breathing and imagery. She had begun to use these techniques for longer periods at home on a daily basis. Once she felt centered, she began an assessment of Mary's "energy flow" by moving her hands slowly from head to foot, a few inches above the skin. When Sue sensed a congestion of energy, she used a sweeping motion to "unruffle" the congestion, then shook her hands as if to rid them of the energy. Next she intentionally "redirected" Mary's energy through visualization and feeling her own energy pass into Mary. Finally, she stopped and "evaluated."   Her goal was to restore balance to Mary's "energy field." The entire procedure took about fifteen minutes.

After the procedure, Mary felt a new sense of closeness to Sue. What is more, Sue felt a deep satisfaction. She had been able to bring comfort in a situation where no further medical or psychological intervention was likely to help. In fact, many Therapeutic Touch practitioners advocate the technique as much for what it does for the nurse as for its effect on patients.

Nurses who practice Therapeutic Touch usually began for some very good reasons. Today's health care system leaves both patients and nurses highly dissatisfied. When cost-effectiveness becomes the ruling factor, the first services to be cut are those that provide the most job satisfaction to nurses—caring measures that take time and adequate personnel to enable them to happen.

Most nurses entered the profession with a desire to serve God and help other people, and they often feel that the ability to do so has been taken away by the current health care system. Therapeutic Touch is one attempt to restore the personal, hands-on approach that both nurses and patients seek.

Most patients today find the changing health care scene confusing, impersonal and frustrating. Drastically reduced time spent in hospitals—and even in follow-up home visits—leaves people alone with their deep fears of suffering and death. Furthermore, many people in our culture are starved for physical touch and intimate relationships. Touch therapies fill those voids by offering extended presence and hope for healing, even in the face of chronic disease or impending death.

Furthermore, Therapeutic Touch seems to work. Anecdotal evidence has convinced a rapidly expanding number of people to try it. Proponents also cite research to confirm the positive effects of Therapeutic Touch. Most major medical centers are beginning to talk about "restoring the mind-body connection," and Therapeutic Touch inevitably becomes part of the picture. What was only recently considered alternative therapy is now becoming mainstream throughout the country.[5]

But Therapeutic Touch and other energy therapies present Christians with some serious problems. Although some Christians do advocate energy-based theories and may practice these therapies with good intentions, they do so naively. The issues include spiritual, ethical and practical concerns.

Dabbling in the occult. In contrast to the biblical worldview, the underlying worldview of most touch therapies involves a belief that impersonal energy can be manipulated and controlled. While in theory the energy is impersonal, many practitioners claim to be in contact with spirits in their meditation time. The therapies themselves are sometimes seen as manipulation of spirits. Some of these therapies claim to be channeled by spirit guides, angels or other entities; others come from roots in Wicca or occult traditions. Christians who were converted out of these belief systems are usually the most adamant against dabbling in them.[6]

Mysticism gone awry. Many proponents of Therapeutic Touch, after practicing the meditative techniques required for the discipline, criticize Christians for ignoring the mystical traditions of the church. The Christian church does have a rich mystical tradition, which became suppressed with the rise of science. We can affirm that there is much in this tradition that should be restored and enjoyed. Mysticism unchecked, however, frequently leads to serious heresy and corruption in the church and blurs the uniqueness of the Christian gospel. Psychologist Elizabeth Hillstrom points out that mystical writers from Maharishi Mahesh Yogi to Christian mystics like St. John of the Cross all warn about the dangers of "madness, demonic deception or possession for those who venture into the mystical path."[7] Richard Foster describes the goal of true Christian mysticism:

> In Meditative Prayer there is no loss of identity, no merging with the cosmic consciousness, no fanciful astral travel. Rather, we are called to life-transforming obedience because we have encountered the living God of Abraham, Isaac, and Jacob. Christ is truly present among us to heal us, to forgive us, to change us, to empower us.[8]

The Bible is the central reference point in Christian mysticism. The mystical experience must always be tested by the Scriptures, not the other way around. When mysticism moves beyond biblical limits, it ceases to be Christian, even when Christian terminology is retained.

Questionable science. From a scientific perspective, proponents of energy-based touch therapies vacillate between two extremes. Some advocates dismiss science entirely and claim the effectiveness of these therapies through anecdotal evidence alone. Others have attempted to use scientific research to measure the effectiveness of Therapeutic Touch. Results, however, remain inconclusive.[9] Although a few advocates have tried to describe this energy as physical (e.g., as electromagnetic fields), most simply assume that it is spiritual and cannot be measured.

An energy-based worldview is not necessary to explain why Therapeutic Touch seems to work. Positive results of Therapeutic Touch and other energy-based therapies can be explained scientifically. For example, human touch, caring presence and a sense of hope can release brain chemicals that promote relaxation and healing. On the other hand, a growing body of research has indicated that the long-term effects of Therapeutic Touch and the meditative states that accompany it may, in fact, be physically and psychologically harmful.[10]

Ethical issues. Furthermore, serious ethical issues arise when using energy-based touch therapies. A clear violation of professional ethics occurs whenever a health care professional uses such a procedure without consent.[11] The ethical issues remain when the person consents but is not fully informed about the rationale or spiritual beliefs behind the procedure. By relating Therapeutic Touch to the church's practice of "laying on of hands,"[12] Sue, the nurse in the case study, misrepresented the therapy and violated her patient's spiritual integrity.

Therapeutic Touch and other energy-based touch therapies

continue to gain adherents in nursing and the general public. Experience is a persuasive teacher. Those who have become convinced of the value of energy-based therapies through their own participation in them will probably not be swayed by these arguments. However, because there are such major theological, ethical and practical issues at stake, Christians must be wary of Therapeutic Touch.

If we believe that Jesus is the only way to salvation and that the gospel is truly good news to sinful humanity, then we need to wake up and take notice of accounts such as one man's experience with energy-based therapy for his problem with tooth-grinding, reported in *Time* magazine. He writes:

> I got more from mind-body medicine than I bargained for. I got religion. . . . The spirituality of it ambushed me. Unwittingly, I was engaging in a practice that has been at the heart of religious mysticism for millenniums. . . . The God I have found is common to Moses and Muhammad, to Buddha and Jesus. . . . It is what the Cabala calls Ayin, Nothingness, No-Thingness. It is Spirit, Being, the All.[13]

Therapeutic Touch is not a neutral technique. In many ways it is idolatry, because it flirts with spiritual powers and systems that God has warned us to shun. It is not an appropriate alternative for Christians, even as a last resort for a dying patient, for in the process of trying to bring temporary comfort we may lead people into spiritually dangerous territory. Instead, in the name of Jesus Christ, we can offer all the resources of the church—a view of reality shaped by the Bible, healing prayer, healthy human relationships that include caring touch, practical support, a worshiping community and the hope of eternal life.

The Christian tradition holds a rich treasure in health and healing. The Bible and the practices of the church point us to the means of grace and the hope of glory, equipping us for the work of healing. The sacraments, prayer, anointing with oil, the laying on of hands, the gifts of the Spirit, and mutual encouragement give us concrete actions to take and the assurance of God's presence with us. Each of these acts directs us to God as the source of healing and hope.

Rather than turning to other belief systems for alternative therapies, Christians need to be acting on and promoting what they already know and have in Christ. Many churches work toward this end by establishing congregational health programs and helping people form supportive relationships (with plenty of hugs). Healing services invite people to come for one-to-one prayer, the laying on of hands and anointing with oil. Lay prayer ministries, as well as pastoral care and deaconal ministries, where church members receive individual attention, provide significant personal support for people facing the reality of suffering. Within the context of healthy relationships in the believing community, people can experience the warmth of intimacy and appropriate physical touch. We can also reach out to those in our care with gentle touch that communicates presence and love.

Part Three

Caring for the Caregiver

9

The Family
Caregiver

Betty *had known the time was coming for several months. Her* mother, Sophie, had grown increasingly confused. Sophie had lived alone and managed quite well for years. Her house and yard always looked immaculate. She especially prided herself on her flowering plants. Until recently, Sophie had watched her younger daughter Alice's children while Alice worked. Then one day her two-year-old grandson Timmy wandered onto the highway. A panicked driver stopped and walked him to the door. Sophie had forgotten Timmy was there.

A week later Sophie got into her car and drove thirty-five miles. When she finally stopped, she did not know where she was or where she had come from. Police notified Alice after finding her phone number on a scrap of paper in Sophie's pocketbook. Finally, Alice called Betty in tears, asking, "What can we *do?*"

Betty was single and was feeling restless in her job. She felt ready for a change and concerned about leaving her mother at home alone. Neither she nor Alice wanted to put their mother into a nursing home at this point. So Betty quit her job in another state and moved three hundred miles back home to care for her mother.

At first things went fairly well. Betty enjoyed having extra time for reading and Bible study. She caught up on dozens of projects that she had ignored while she was working. She found interesting things to do around the house, and she helped Sophie maintain her flowers and shrubs. Although Betty quickly tired of hearing the same stories over and over again, she learned to mentally turn off her hearing and feign interest. It did annoy her when she told her mother something important, only to be asked ten minutes later about the same thing. But most of the time Sophie was pleasant and easy to handle. Betty would take Sophie out shopping, visiting and to church.

As Sophie's condition continued to deteriorate, she did not have the physical stamina to walk far. A wheelchair helped for a while, but soon her behavior became disruptive in public situations. Betty stopped going out except when Alice could relieve her for a few hours. With Alice's full-time job and active family, though, those times were limited.

Betty began to feel like a prisoner in her own home. She had few friends in the community, and all of them worked full-time. Even her church seemed like a different place from before she moved away twenty years ago. The pastor stopped by to visit once, but Betty did not feel that she knew him well enough to share her concerns with him. Caring for her mother made it difficult to become involved with any small group activities at church or to establish relationships with others in the congregation. Even the neighbors were new, and they kept to themselves.

How many "Bettys" do you know? In this time of managed

care, with its decreasing benefits, a large number of family caregivers are finding themselves feeling stuck at home, shouldering a heavy burden alone. Galatians tells us, "Bear one another's burdens, and in this way you will fulfill the law of Christ" (6:2). The "law of Christ" is clearly stated by Jesus: "'You shall love the Lord your God with all your heart, and with all your soul, and with all your mind.' This is the greatest and first commandment. And a second is like it: 'You shall love your neighbor as yourself'" (Mt 22:37-39).

How can we love the family caregivers in our congregation and our community as we love ourselves? There are some concrete actions we can take to show them love, but all of them call for a high level of compassion and commitment. First, we can offer respite—providing a few hours when the caregiver can get away. Second, we can provide friendship and support. Third, we can help caregivers recognize their own needs as well as the needs of the person in their care. Fourth, we can become aware of resources within the church and the community to meet the needs that we assess.

Offering Respite

Elaine was a widow in her mid-sixties who cared for her ninety-year-old mother, Harriet, after a stroke. It was hard physical work. The stroke had paralyzed Harriet's left side and affected her speech and emotions. Although she could speak, many of her words were inappropriate and hard to understand. When Elaine did not respond immediately to her every request, she would bang on the table, shouting at Elaine, then sob uncontrollably. Elaine found herself responding in kind, and she hated herself for doing it.

On one particularly difficult day, Bob and Ginny, a couple who had been long-time friends with Elaine and her husband, stopped by to visit. Elaine poured out her frustrations to them. Then Harriet demanded that Elaine come back to her bedroom to tend to her. While Elaine was out of the room Bob and Ginny discussed her situation. It felt so familiar to them. They had cared for Bob's mother in their home for years, facing similar frustrations. They came up with a plan.

When Elaine returned, apologizing profusely, Bob told her, "Elaine, we think we can help. We cared for my mom, so we're not intimidated by your mother's needs. We've also known her most of our lives, so I don't think she'd feel uncomfortable around us. We don't have any plans for this afternoon. Why don't you just get in your car and go shopping, or do whatever you want to do for a couple of hours. We'll stay here while you're gone. What's more, we'd like to do this every Tuesday afternoon, if that's okay with you."

Getting away made Elaine feel like a different person. She experienced a new sense of freedom and could reset her emotional reactions. When she came home, she could be more patient with her mother. The hope for another respite the following week kept her going. Suddenly she no longer felt trapped.

Mark Henry, pastor of St. James Church, developed another approach to providing respite through the church. He knew of several family caregivers tending elderly parents or spouses with Alzheimer's, and all of them felt trapped and frustrated. Mark organized a cooperative respite at the church, along with a group of women who met weekly to quilt. The quilters served lunch and light refreshments, as well as organizing simple entertainment such as hymn sings, barbershop quartets and programs by children from the church preschool. The caregivers brought their charges and took turns either staying to assist with care or having the time free. Those who stayed appreciated the time with other caregivers and a break from the monotony of the daily routine.

The need for respite also becomes crucial in families with disabled children. Linda Treloar, mother of a disabled daughter, explains:

> We relocated to Arizona when Joy was ten. Although the warmer climate allowed more freedom of movement for our daughter in a motorized wheelchair, little else encouraged positive growth in our family. Through the years, we seldom had a date, an evening out or a vacation. Why? Because persons with disabilities have physical care needs which often require lifting and use of special equipment. People are fearful that their caregiving skills are inadequate, or that they will hurt themselves in lifting the person with disabilities. Families fear that a caregiver could sue them should an injury or alleged injury occur.
>
> Respite services, if they are available, are extremely limited. They may or may not involve care in the person's home. They may involve the services of a sitter, without any actual physical care. To hire agency-supplied caregivers for respite is beyond the financial capabilities of the average family. Unless the family has an extended support system with individuals willing and able to provide needed services to allow able-bodied family members to leave for an evening out or for a short vacation, it doesn't occur. My dream is that someday churches will reach out to families with disabled members in a very concrete way, by providing low-cost respite services.[1]

What *can* churches and communities do to provide respite? The concerns Linda expresses are very real—for those volunteering to help, as well as for the families. When my father was homebound following a stroke, his friend Gene came faithfully every week to take him to Rotary meetings. It was a wonderful break for my mother, but Daddy required help transferring to and from a wheelchair. One day Gene wrenched his back trying to help Daddy into the car. His back strain took months to heal, so Gene stopped offering rides. Caring for disabled people requires knowledge and skill. Churches could also be legally liable if either a volunteer caregiver or the disabled person was injured. Parish nurses may be able to teach proper transfer techniques to family caregivers, as well as instructing volunteers about legal limitations for their involvement.

Churches and church-related agencies in many areas do provide limited respite help, but that does not usually include physical care. The agency affiliated with my own church provides rides to medical appointments, shopping, companionship, meals and spiritual support, but cannot offer any physical care. However, even such limited services can be a tremendous relief to overburdened caregivers. Volunteers receive a brief orientation and training, and most of them feel a deep sense of commitment and fulfillment in their ministry.

Some churches have actually started their own home care agencies with Christian nurses and home health aides from the congregation. Sometimes nurses within the congregation, especially those not employed in nursing full-time, will eagerly volunteer to provide short-term care. Perhaps a wiser approach, rather than trying to provide direct services that require professional expertise or extensive training, would be to develop a fund so that the church could offer certificates for an occasional "free night out," paying the bill for a caregiver from a nursing service.

Groups such as Handi*Vangelism and JAF Ministries[2] provide wonderful opportunities for children with disabilities to attend summer camps and retreats. Parents can get away for a real vacation while their children enjoy being with other children in a safe environment.

Avoiding Isolation

Most caregivers eventually find themselves isolated from friends, neighbors and the outside world in general. Caregiving consumes not only all their time but their thoughts and emotions as well. A confusing mix of compassion and anger may compound the isolation. Old friendships may feel awkward and uncomfortable as caregivers lose themselves in caregiving. The freedom and apparently trouble-free lives of their friends may spark jealousy and disdain in caregivers.

Ellen belonged to a group of women who met monthly for lunch. They usually worked on a craft project and spent some time praying together. When Ellen's husband, Herb, became disabled after an automobile accident, the group went out of their way to include Ellen. Sometimes one of the other husbands would stay with Herb so Ellen could get away. At other times the group met at Herb and Ellen's house. As time went on, however, Ellen found she had little to talk about with her friends. They were busy going places with their husbands and other companions. Conversation usually turned to their latest cruise or plans for the next exciting venture. Ellen's routine seldom changed. She cared for Herb every day. The days all blended together into a long, tedious routine. Her world no longer stretched beyond the borders of her house or an occasional trip to the drugstore or supermarket. Finally Ellen told her friends that she no longer wanted to meet with them.

Ellen's outlook changed radically, though, when she began meeting with a caregivers' support group at a neighboring church. For the first time she found other people who were experiencing the same feelings and situations. She poured out her heart, only to find that everyone in the room could identify with the things she was facing. They also shared their own stories, including the ways they had worked through difficulties, found resources for help and overcome their own anger and resentment. They also prayed for one another in a way that only someone who truly understood could pray. The group helped Ellen see that getting out and doing things that she enjoyed would really help Herb in the long run, because it would refresh her to care for him without the resentment her self-imposed isolation created.

Where can you find a support group? Many local hospitals, organizations and churches have support groups in place for caregivers as well as for those suffering from various conditions, including Alzheimer's, chronic disabilities, drug and substance abuse, AIDS/HIV, multiple sclerosis, chronic fatigue, mental illness and cancer. You can usually locate them fairly quickly by contacting your pastor, parish nurse or hospital or by looking in the "blue pages" of your local phone directory. A Christian support group will be especially helpful, because caregivers will find prayer support and biblical encouragement as well as peer support. However, any support group is better than none at all.

If no caregivers' support groups exist to meet the need in your community, consider starting one. The first step is to identify the need. Who might benefit from this group? List the people you think might appreciate a support group. Talk with them to discern their interests and concerns. Next, enlist others to help. You will need a facilitator with skills and training in leading support groups, as well as a group of volunteers to provide respite care while the caregivers are meeting. You will also want to find resource people in the community who can provide education and links to other services in the area. Some caregivers may need transportation. Some may not drive; others will hesitate to venture out alone. Once the support group is organized, advertise through church bulletins and newsletters, visiting nurse and other home care agencies, hospitals and doctors' offices.

Recognizing Needs

When Ken and Lisa first agreed to become foster parents for eight-year-old Melissa, the whole congregation supported them eagerly. Melissa came from a home where she had been sexually abused. She was severely autistic and required constant attention. She arrived with only the torn, soiled clothing that she was wearing. When word spread, the church collected a large supply of used clothing and some lovely new outfits for Melissa. One Sunday-school teacher, who was certified in special education, agreed to work with Melissa individually and attempted to integrate her into the primary class.

Melissa did not cooperate. She frightened the other children in Sunday school. Several of them stopped coming. Those who remained were not kind. Finally Lisa decided that it was not fair to disrupt the entire primary department with Melissa's behavior. She kept her at home, alternating Sundays with Ken. But neither Lisa nor Ken liked attending worship alone, so finally both stopped coming to church. Their commitment to Melissa continued, and they finally adopted her, but no one at the church even knew.

All too often caregivers quietly drift away from the church community. It just takes too much effort to attend worship and participate in church activities. The old adage "out of sight, out of mind" comes true more often than not. Several years ago I served on a committee that was considering how to make our church buildings more convenient and accessible to people with disabilities. One committee member spoke up for many in the congregation, asking, "Why do we need to have ramps? We don't have anyone attending worship in a wheelchair!" Of course we didn't—they couldn't get into the building if they did come.

Needs of disabled people and their caregivers may not be obvious. Many simply stop coming. Others put up a good front. They work hard to get to church every Sunday, so no one looks at them as particularly needy. Sometimes they grow increasingly ornery and cryptic, so others tend to avoid them.

Christian caregivers often face the additional burden of guilt: they think it is selfish and un-Christian to take care of their own needs in the face of the overwhelming needs of others. Part of the challenge in recognizing needs of caregivers comes in establishing a supportive climate where they will feel safe in communicating their anger, frustration and personal needs.

Here are some good ways to help the weary caregivers you know:

1. Visit families dealing with chronic illness or disability when they stop attending church events. Go often, and keep going. Listen carefully, and provide spiritual care. Often, when you suspect a need or concern, you can mention it in prayer. For instance, if you are sensing that a caregiver is feeling guilty over his impatience with his demanding, sick wife, you could pray, "We thank you, Lord, that you understand how hard it is to care for someone day in and day out without getting impatient. . . ." That gives the caregiver permission to share his feelings. He knows you won't be shocked or condemning.

2. Provide safe opportunities for caregivers who do attend church to share honestly. On the first Sunday of each month, several nurses in the congregation set up blood pressure screening stations in the Sunday-school classrooms after the worship service. While monitoring blood pressures is important, the conversation that accompanies it outweighs any physical benefits. It provides an opportunity for people to talk about their deepest health-related concerns.

Many times caregivers come to discuss their family member's health needs but end up expressing their own. We end up discussing options and considering alternatives.

3. Don't hesitate to ask, "How can I help you?" You may have to be more specific and offer some alternatives: "Could I stay with Joe while you go to the store?" "Can I pick up some groceries for you?" "We're having a great stew tonight, and I've made too much. May I bring some over for you and Esther?" "How can I pray for you today?"

4. Read materials that will help you understand the person's needs. Books written by people who have lived through similar experiences—especially those whose faith has helped them—and brochures from the Cancer Society, Heart Association or other reputable organizations will enable you to anticipate needs. When shared sensitively with caregivers, they can provide helpful talking points. For example, you could say, "This pamphlet mentions that caregivers often feel overwhelmed. Do you ever feel that way?"

5. Know when to pull back. When others recognize your helpfulness and generosity, you too may become overwhelmed. Learn to set limits—know that you can say no. Find reinforcements so you won't be doing all the work yourself. Ministering to others may give you a sense of joy and fulfillment, but you also need to plan for fun and relaxation. And don't slight your own family and friends when caring for others.

Sources of Help

Most of all, remember that you are not alone. Become familiar with the resources in your community. Get to know the individuals in charge of various community services so that you can refer people to them appropriately. Help them get connected. You may want to look for a support group for yourself. Parish nurses usually meet for support on a regular basis. These groups are often organized by local hospitals, churches or the nurses themselves. Nurses Christian Fellowship[3] groups meet for Bible study and prayer, as well as continuing education. Community volunteer agencies often have monthly meetings where volunteers can discuss concerns and support one another. Churches with organized volunteer ministries, such as Stephen Ministers,[4] will usually offer opportunities for prayer, Bible study and further training.

After looking for local support groups, resources and services, you may want to explore national and international organizations that offer help for caregivers. The Internet opens a vast array of opportunities that increases almost daily. You can search for support groups, gather information about particular conditions and organizations, and enter into "chat rooms" with others who share your concerns. However, you can also find a lot of unreliable information and strange treatments, so keep your discernment skills sharp.

The following Christian organizations provide both written resources and opportunities for learning and support:

Christian Recovery International
P.O. Box 11095
Whittier, CA 90605
(310) 690-9701
Provides support groups, seminars and workshops for families in stress. They also produce a quarterly magazine, *Steps*.

BCM International
237 Fairfield Avenue
Upper Darby, PA 19082
(610) 352-7177

Provides training programs for working with children, teens and young adults with disabilities; Handi*Camp for children who are disabled; Parents in Progress, a support group for parents of disabled children; and many other programs and resources, including books and newsletters for caregivers and people with disabilities.

JAF Ministries
P.O. Box 3333
Agoura Hills, CA 91301
(818) 707-5664

Sponsors retreats for families with disabled children, support groups and many resources for those dealing with chronic disability.

10

Caring for Yourself

Kevin *sank into the living room sofa exhausted. The previous week* had seemed endless and filled with crises. He had not had a full night's sleep all week. The only flight nurse at Memorial Hospital, Kevin had remained on call twenty-four hours a day. He had worked for nine days without a break and been awakened every night for emergencies. One accident scene in particular continued to haunt him. Five high-school seniors in a compact car slammed into a tractor-trailer at high speed. Three were killed instantly, but the two who were Medevac'd to the trauma center were in critical condition. One died the following day, but the other, Jimmy Malloy, remained on the edge of eternity. Both of these teens were from Kevin's church. Kevin rode in the helicopter with the two boys. He continued to visit Jimmy daily and to support both sets of frightened, grieving parents.

As Kevin reached for the TV remote, both of his preschool children bounded into the room and plopped onto his lap. "Daddy, come and see my bunny!" four-year-old Amanda demanded.

"Nobody will push me in the swing," whined three-year-old Nathan.

"Honey, we're out of milk—can you run to the store and get a gallon before dinner?" his wife, Megan, called from the kitchen.

Kevin groaned inwardly as he asked the children if they wanted to go for a ride. He had a deacons' meeting at church after dinner, and he really just wanted to withdraw and relax for a few minutes before dinner. That did not seem to be an option.

Kevin dreaded the deacons' meeting. He knew the other deacons would be pressing him for details about the crash and Jimmy's condition. If Jimmy survived, he would be severely disabled. Kevin didn't even want to think about it, but it was the deacons' responsibility to minister to Jimmy and his family, so he would have to pull himself together in order to guide and support the others.

When Kevin finally dragged himself to the deacons' meeting ten minutes late, they were already deep in discussion. Conversation ceased as he entered the room. Two of the deacons met him at the door and embraced him. After Kevin settled into a chair, Randy, the head deacon, looked at him compassionately. "Kevin, this has been a difficult week for you—how are you doing?" Kevin related the events of the preceding days, then began to weep.

His friends listened patiently and encouraged him to keep talking. Finally Randy suggested that they all gather around Kevin to lay hands on him and pray. Afterward they began to work out a plan for sharing the load of supporting the Malloys and the parents of the boy who died. Kevin went home exhausted but strangely refreshed. He knew he was not alone. There were people caring for him and supporting him in his ministry.

Finding Support in the Worshiping Community

Most North American Christians have grown up valuing rugged individualism and autonomy. Although the Scriptures do emphasize the *personal* nature of faith, God never intended for it to be an *independent* practice. There is no such thing as an autonomous Christian. We are called to community, to *shalom*.

When we look in on the early Christians, we see them responding to crisis as a body. After the death of Jesus his fearful disciples huddled together in one room. "When it was evening on that day, the first day of the week, and the doors of the house where the disciples had met were locked for fear of the Jews, Jesus came and stood among them and said, 'Peace *[shalom]* be with you'" (Jn 20:19).

Being together in their despair provided emotional support; more than that, it prepared them to see Jesus. Had Jesus appeared only to an isolated individual or two, the others might not have believed their report. Furthermore, after the flush of the moment wore off, those who saw him while they were alone might have convinced themselves that their imagination was going wild—perhaps this was only wishful thinking. Experiencing God's presence in the assembled body provides consensual validation to our faith events and reinforces their reality. We tend to get caught up in the urgency of everyday life and lose sight of God's presence and priorities. Being together in the worshiping community renews our hope.

It was probably that very need that drew those disciples together in the days that followed. The story continues in the book of Acts. "When the day of Pentecost had come, they were all together in one place. And suddenly from heaven there came a sound like the rush of a violent wind, and it filled the entire house where they were sitting. Divided tongues, as of fire, appeared among them, and a tongue rested on each of them. All of them were filled with the Holy Spirit and began to speak in other languages, as the Spirit gave them ability" (Acts 2:1-4). It was while they were *together* in that place they received the power to go out to minister in Christ's name. We need the worshiping community to receive the strength and inspiration of the Holy Spirit in order to care for others.

That ministry frequently got the early disciples into big trouble. In Acts 4, Peter and John had been arrested for teaching and healing in Jesus' name. After they were released from custody, they immediately went to their friends and reported that the chief priests and the elders had warned them not to speak of Jesus again.

> When they heard it, they raised their voices together to God and said, "Sovereign Lord, who made the heaven and the earth, the sea, and everything in them, it is you who said by the Holy Spirit through our ancestor David, your servant:
>
> Why did the Gentiles rage,
>   and the peoples imagine vain things?
> The kings of the earth took their stand,
>   and the rulers have gathered together
> against the Lord and against his Messiah.
>
> For in this city, in fact, both Herod and Pontius Pilate, with the Gentiles and the peoples of Israel, gathered together against your holy servant Jesus, whom you anointed, to do whatever your hand and your plan had predestined to take place. And now, Lord, look at their threats, and grant to your servants to speak your word with all boldness, while you stretch out your hand to heal, and signs and wonders are performed through the name of your holy servant Jesus." When they had prayed, the place in which they were gathered together was shaken; and they were all filled with the Holy

Spirit and spoke the word of God with boldness.

Now the whole group of those who believed were of one heart and soul, and no one claimed private ownership of any possessions, but everything they owned was held in common. With great power the apostles gave their testimony to the resurrection of the Lord Jesus, and great grace was upon them all. There was not a needy person among them, for as many as owned lands or houses sold them and brought the proceeds of what was sold. They laid it at the apostles' feet, and it was distributed to each as any had need. (Acts 4:24-35)

What was going on in this community? First, it was a *haven of refuge*. Peter and John knew that they would find support for themselves and their ministry among the gathered church. They were welcomed and sheltered. Second, they were immediately supported in *prayer*. This prayer not only petitioned God for help but acknowledged his power and promises while recalling his track record. That alone would provide perspective and encouragement. Third, they appealed to *Scripture*, focusing their attention on an objective word from the Lord rather than their own perceptions of reality. Fourth, they corporately experienced the *power of the Holy Spirit*. This was no holy huddle! The boldness that got Peter and John into trouble with the law became contagious. They came seeking refuge but ended up going out with an empowered team. Finally, they took care of one another's *physical needs*. This was a holistic community, not a "Sunday-go-to-meeting" crowd. They were sensitive to one another's needs and provided what was needed to support one another—in their daily lives as well as in ministry.

As the story unfolds in the book of Acts, we see this caring community spreading to other areas. As Paul prepared to leave Ephesus, he met with church elders on the beach. "When he had finished speaking, he knelt down with them all and prayed. There was much weeping among them all; they embraced Paul and kissed him, grieving especially because of what he had said, that they would not see him again. Then they brought him to the ship" (Acts 20:36-38).

If we are to care for the spiritual needs of others, we must find a community to encourage and sustain us in ministry. If you do not already belong to such a community, begin to look for a small group that meets regularly. You may have to start one yourself. Within your own congregation you can develop a caregivers' support group for Bible study, prayer and sharing. Nurses Christian Fellowship (NCF) groups meet around the world. NCF also provides Bible study guides, books, the *Journal of Christian Nursing,* continuing education and retreats for nurses.[1] Other possibilities include parish nurse support groups, Stephen Ministries, Nurses for Christ, Hospital Christian Fellowship and denominational ministry support groups. Whatever you do, don't try to do any kind of caring ministry all by yourself.

Finding a Mentor

In addition to the worshiping community as a whole, we also see a pattern in the New Testament of more experienced Christians mentoring younger ones. Wherever the apostle Paul traveled, he took others with him for fellowship and training—Barnabas, Silas, Priscilla and Aquila, Timothy, Phoebe, and a host of others. He also kept in touch with them through writing, instructing Timothy by letter, "and what you have heard from me through many witnesses entrust to faithful people who will be able to teach others as well" (2 Tim 2:2).

Ideally, a mentor should be a more mature Christian whom you see often, for most of what we learn from mentors is "caught, not taught." But mentoring doesn't just happen; it is an intentional relationship in which the mentor takes that role seriously, looking for opportunities to guide, nurture and correct when necessary. The person being mentored also takes the relationship seriously, seeking guidance, sharing concerns and asking for critiques.

Sandy has been my mentor in teaching. I have watched her teach others, and I've been intrigued with her use of illustrations and her ability to skillfully guide a discussion through reflective questions. She cares deeply for her students and often goes far beyond what is expected to enable them to succeed. Her students hold her in great respect. Though we are now colleagues, I have also been her student. As I taught my first graduate course, Sandy attended the classes, and after each one we evaluated my teaching together. She encouraged me in what I had done well and challenged me to improve in other areas. As I graded papers for the first time, she listened as I weighed the merits and weaknesses of each paper and struggled to determine a fair grade. She never told me what to do, but she helped me to consider all the factors involved, then supported me in those difficult decisions.

Finding a mentor in spiritual care will ease the apprehension you may be feeling. Jill asked me to mentor her when we worked together as nurses. Jill was a committed Christian, but she had never prayed with a patient or had the courage to discuss spiritual concerns at work. I began by inviting her to join me as I checked on Miriam, a sixty-year-old woman with metastatic breast cancer. We adjusted Miriam's sheets, checked her IV and stopped to talk. Miriam was obviously in pain, although she had just received a dose of the prescribed analgesic. I held her hand gently and asked how she was feeling. She moaned and said, "I wish the Lord would just take me home." I picked up on her comment and we continued to discuss her relationship with the Lord and how her faith had sustained her through these difficult days. Then I offered to pray for her at the bedside.

After we left the room, Jill remarked, "That was so easy! I think I could do that—I just never thought it was acceptable in a professional situation."

The next day, Jill had to suction Hilda's new tracheostomy. Hilda was highly anxious and seemed to be grasping for control, making the whole procedure difficult. Jill carefully explained each step, but Hilda kept grabbing her hand and pushing it away whenever she attempted to suction. All the while, the mucus in her trachea rattled dangerously. Finally, Jill asked, "Would it help if I prayed for both of us as I do this?" Hilda nodded forcefully. Jill held her hand and prayed aloud, asking God to help them both relax. Hilda calmed noticeably, and Jill was able to quickly suction the mucus, to Hilda's great relief.

Afterward, Jill found me at the nurses' station and reported, her eyes dancing, "I did it! I did it! And it wasn't hard!" She recounted the whole event. In the process of reviewing what happened, she thought of how she might have approached Hilda differently at the beginning of the encounter—and marveled at the way prayer changed their interaction. As Jill became more comfortable with spiritual care, she and I would discuss various approaches at the nurses' station. Other staff began to listen in on our discussions, and they too became involved in offering spiritual care.

In mentoring, life and everyday experiences become the textbook. There is no set curriculum, although there may be boundaries. Mentors don't meddle; they model. For the most part, the mentee sets the agenda, but the mentor shares wisdom gleaned from experience. Sometimes the mentor-mentee relationship will become a two-way proposition. For example, Lynn, a new graduate nurse, asked Millie to be her mentor in nursing. Millie had been a nurse for thiry years, but she was a relatively new Christian. Lynn had been a Christian since childhood and was spiritually mature for her age, so Millie asked Lynn to mentor *her* in her faith. They meet every Saturday morning for coffee to review their week and learn from one another, study the Bible and pray.

Technology has made long-distance mentoring possible as well. I have a friend in Korea who asked me to be her mentor. We rarely see each other in person, but we communicate frequently through e-mail. She sends me her goals to review and writes about situations she is facing. I ask questions, make occasional suggestions and offer resources. I also have several e-mail mentors, people I respect to whom I can send off a quick message to gain rapid feedback when facing a difficult situation.

E-mail has several advantages. A written message allows the mentor to think and pray before responding. It also may communicate more clearly than spontaneous conversation; however, there will be times when the human voice or physical presence seems essential. E-mail does not communicate human emotions well. It can be terse and blunt. When emotions flare, it is time to pick up the phone or arrange a face-to-face meeting.

Telephone mentoring, though more expensive than e-mail, may be more comfortable for those who prefer verbal communication. My friend Skip lives a thousand miles away, but she asked me to be her mentor and prayer partner. We meet by phone every Wednesday morning to review our weeks, talk and pray. She is also a budding writer, so I have now agreed to work with her by mail and e-mail to develop her writing skills.

Who are your mentors? If you do not have one, who are the people you admire—especially those who have skills you would like to develop? Consider asking one to be your mentor. Set some goals for your time together. Figure out what you want to learn from your mentor and how you would like to learn. Will you go with your mentor to observe her in action? Would you like him to observe you in action? Will you keep a journal to review together? Will you pray and study Scripture or merely meet to talk? Determine a regular time and place to meet. You may also want to decide on a time span to set some parameters to the commitment. Will the mentoring relationship last six months? a year? indefinitely?

Stop now and pray about whether the Lord wants you to become involved in a mentoring relationship. As the names of potential mentors come to mind, pray for them and ask God to guide you to the right person. Prayerfully set some goals. Then take the big step and ask one person to mentor you.

Taking Care of Yourself

Although we are all interdependent and function as a body, each of us has a particular responsibility to care for ourselves. Maybe we can learn something from the instructions of the airline flight attendants who tell us, "In case of an emergency, an oxygen mask will fall from the overhead compartment—please be sure your own mask is in place before assisting someone else." An oxygen-deprived or dead caregiver will not be much help to anyone else. In the same way, when we are depleted physically, emotionally or spiritually, we cannot care for others effectively. When Jesus commanded, "You shall love your neighbor as yourself" (Mt 22:39), he assumed that we would love ourselves. Loving ourselves involves caring for our own physical, emotional, mental and spiritual needs.

First, we need to look after our *physical health*—doing those things our mothers drilled into us, like eating right, getting enough sleep, exercising and getting regular medical and dental checkups. I can always tell when I've violated those principles. Sometimes, when pressures and deadlines begin to mount, I force myself to sit at the computer for long hours cranking out the work. I don't have time to fix nourishing meals, so we go out for fast food. Exercise doesn't happen. My mind continues to race after I go to bed. My morning devotional time slips into thinking about my "to do" list. Before long I start getting ornery with my family and friends, my blood pressure and weight begin to creep up, and my back ends up in a painful knot. In that shape I'm not much good to anyone. Believe me, taking care of your own physical needs is a favor to those you love and serve.

Emotional needs are closely tied with physical needs. An abused body will throw a person into depression, increase anxiety and set off a cycle of feelings and behavior that then further damage physical health. At a time in my life when I was struggling with some serious medical problems, I began to focus so much on the illness that it seemed to consume my life. A good friend gently reminded me, "Judy, it's spring—get out and smell the tulips!" I began to walk outdoors several miles a day, enjoying the beauty that surrounded me, talking to God and breathing the fresh air. Before long my perspective returned and I sensed God's presence again. Physical healing began as well.

Caring for our emotional needs includes living a balanced life. Setting aside time for recreation is not frivolous; we need to play as well as work. In spite of Jesus' heavy ministry schedule, he took time to hang out with friends, enjoy parties and go off into the wilderness alone. He knew how to say no in order to say yes to the right things.

My friend Jeff tells about a time when he found himself in a major emotional slump. He just couldn't work up any enthusiasm for ministry, but he kept going through the motions. The harder he worked, the less successful he felt, so he worked harder. He felt guilty, so he spent hours in prayer, confessing his overwhelming sense of failure. He spent extra time in Bible study and reading motivational books. Nothing helped. Finally his next-door neighbor, an avowed atheist, cajoled him into joining a neighborhood basketball league. Jeff loved basketball but hadn't played in years. He justified joining the team by considering it an evangelism effort. After playing the first game Jeff felt exhilarated—and exhausted. He went home and slept more soundly than he had in months, and he woke up feeling like a new person.

What do you love to do for recreation? Put it into your calendar, and plan ahead so you will do it. Even when work and volunteer activities seem to be consuming you, make time for fun, family, friendship and personal refreshment.

When emotional needs are deep-seated or severe, counseling will be necessary. When getting our basic needs met or changing our circumstances doesn't lift us out of emotional struggles, it is time for professional help. Even Christians become clinically depressed and suffer a host of mental and emotional illnesses. That is not a sign of weakness or sin. It is a demonstration of strength and wisdom to get the needed help to cope with these conditions.

We also have *intellectual needs* that must be met if we are to function effectively. We should never stop intentionally learning. Think about how you learn best, and set some concrete goals that will prepare you for your ministry as well as bring you enjoyment. Take a class on caregiving or gardening. Read books and periodicals. Think carefully about which periodicals you should be reading regularly. Listen to an audiotape series as you drive. Watch a video that will expand your knowledge or make you laugh. People with few outside interests are not much fun to be around. Enjoy learning! At the same time, you may find that your interest in model trains or cultivating roses opens the door to ministry with someone who shares your passion.

Finally, we must maintain a healthy *spiritual life* in order to meet the spiritual needs of others. We are a work-oriented culture. I usually feel guilty when I rest and righteous when I work hard. The virtue of work was drilled into me as a child. I was praised for studying, but when I sat around reading a book for pleasure I was told to do something constructive. Our peers reinforce our work ethic. If someone asks how we are, we proudly complain, "I've been so busy lately!" But God does not applaud our self-righteous enslavement to work. Instead, according to Isaiah 30:15, "In returning and rest you shall be saved; in quietness and in trust shall be your strength."

Where are we to return? First of all, to God, of course. We become so intent on our busyness that we neglect to take adequate time for prayer, Bible reading and worship. Martin Luther once said, "I have so much to do that I cannot get on without three hours a day of praying." Most of us tend to think just the opposite. But how often do we end up spinning our wheels in useless activity because we never bothered to consult the Lord about what was important in his eyes?

Sometimes the returning needs to be to the people around us. We need to be present to them, listening to them, caring for them, instead of running off with our own agenda. It is so easy to make a big project of caring for someone, when all they really wanted was five minutes of our undivided attention.

We are also to return to rest. Rest, without feeling guilty. God wants us to stop doing and fixing for a while. He knows that our minds and bodies need time to be refreshed and restored. He made us that way. We are cheating ourselves and God when we ignore his commandment to keep the sabbath. In fact, our work becomes more productive when we get serious about taking adequate rest. Christians throughout history have found that this rest in the Lord needs to be both a daily time of personal devotion and a periodical withdrawing for a more extended time of retreat.

Daily devotions begin with a commitment to the Lord to meet him for a set period of time every day. For many Christians the quiet time at the beginning of the day works best, but others prefer evening or that brief stillness while the children are napping. Here is one suggested plan for your quiet time that has worked well for many people.

Begin with a time of *praise* and reflection. A psalm or hymn may help to focus your attention.

Read a manageable portion of Scripture—anything from one verse to a chapter. A devotional guide may be helpful in directing your reading. Don't try to make your devotional period into a contest to see how many books of the Bible you can read in a year. Save that kind of Bible reading for another time. This is a time of fellowship with God, a time to listen to what he is saying to you for this day.

Meditate on what you have read. What is God saying to you about himself? his promises? his people? What direction does the passage give to you? Does it point to sin that needs confessing? a task to be done? an attitude to change? What does the passage say about the world around you? How can it help you to understand reality? make decisions? serve more appropriately?

Finally, turn to God in *prayer.* The acronym *ACTS* has helped many in organizing this time of prayer. *Adoration* includes praise, enjoyment and appreciation expressed to God for his character. *Confession* involves taking our sin to God and laying it at his feet so that we can be forgiven and restored. *Thanksgiving* differs from adoration; it focuses on what God has done rather than on who he is. It is a recognition of our gratitude for his presence and activity in our lives. *Supplication* means bringing our concerns to God: our requests for ourselves, our loved ones and others.

Times of extended retreat may be based on the same format, but with more time to focus on each aspect. I like to spend a day in prayer at home about once a month. Sometimes I will go off into the woods or to a church by myself. I take a Bible, hymnal and note pad. Those times apart usually refocus my priorities and lead to more productive work in the days ahead.

Other opportunities for spiritual refreshment include organized retreats and time at a retreat center for a silent retreat. Many retreat centers provide spiritual directors to offer personal guidance for your time alone with God.

Healthy spiritual growth requires both private time with God and the fellowship of other believers. Neither is sufficient alone. If we merely keep our faith private, we cannot be vibrantly attached to the body. The opposite danger is to become so caught up in the social aspects of fellowship and service that we miss that personal relationship with God entirely.

Our relationship with God is similar to a marriage. If a couple does not relate to others, they become ingrown. God wants to meet our needs through other people—and expects us to care for them as well. On the other hand, if a couple is constantly involved in group activities or running in opposite directions all day, not guarding personal time for intimacy, their relationship soon deteriorates. God wants us to be balanced, whole people who live in close relationship with him and with one another.

11

Developing a
Spiritual Care
Team

W*hy does everyone call me when they need help?" Kristin spoke* aloud to no one in particular as she hung up the phone. This was supposed to be her one day off this week, but by ten o'clock the whole day was already full. She was planning to take the tape of Sunday's worship service to three shut-ins, visit two friends in the hospital and bake a cake for a funeral the next day. Now her next-door neighbor, Barb, was in crisis over her dissolving marriage. She invited Barb to lunch, but she had no idea what she would serve. Kristin felt that God had given her the gift of "helps," but she was beginning to wonder how to balance the overwhelming barrage of opportunities.

Sometimes we create our own stress by being competent and dependable. At other times we have no control over the stressors that come our way. However, there are ways to cope, and even thrive, in the midst of multiple responsibilities. My friend Sylvia wrote, "Since we returned from vacation last month, our ninety-year-old aunt had a massive stroke and went home to be with the Lord, so we went to her funeral in Maine. When we got back I faced heavy teaching responsibilities at work on top of writing four major grant proposals. Now we are in 'panic city' about our upcoming accreditation review next month. I sometimes long for the old days of being young, naive and irresponsible. Now, everyone sees me as the 'rock' and integral to all the functions in the program—a very, very hard expectation to meet. Through tribulation comes patience."

In the same message, though, Sylvia described her work with a team of volunteers she coordinates. Nurturing and encouraging the volunteer team had not been an easy task. Most of the volunteers were inexperienced, and even those who should have known what to do seemed to have difficulty following directions. It might have been easier to do the job herself, but Sylvia had patience, allowing them to almost fail. In the end she delighted in each team member's contribution. She wrote, "Andrea's focused attention to detail is a real strength for the team. Cindy's artistic tastefulness and personal, joyous interactional style are a ballet! Monica's love for nurses and her strong interpersonal relations with each individual she contacts for Christ is a wonder to behold. They all do an excellent job keeping people nourished and comfortable. We should probably do another project in the spring."

Sylvia is already planning how to help the team learn from their mistakes and build on their strengths. She is also keeping her perspective through participating in group Bible study and enlisting others to pray with her. She also finds support through networking with other volunteer leaders and seeking their counsel.

Organizing Volunteers

The first step in avoiding "compassion fatigue" is to develop a plan for sharing the load. Yet most of us respond to cries for help as Kristin did. It's flattering when someone asks you for help. You feel honored and needed. Helping people gives you a sense of meaning, purpose and fulfillment—and wins praises from others. This dynamic tends to feed on itself and tap into your sense of pride. Eventually helping others becomes addictive—the need-to-be-needed syndrome. Sharing the load can be tough at first, especially if you are responsible.

Sylvia is a wise and mature leader, but some of her friends and colleagues became annoyed when her recent project began to run into problems. As they sat back and criticized her "lack of leadership," I'm sure she fought the urge to just take over and do everything herself. Instead, she patiently coached Andrea, Cindy and Monica. She listened, guided, evaluated and demonstrated over and over again. Now the volunteer team has a success to enjoy, and next year's project will be easier.

Organizing volunteers to provide spiritual care requires careful assessment and planning, as well as vision, training and ongoing encouragement. Even before the recruiting begins, you will need to determine all the aspects of the ministry you envision. Next, consider the gifts, skills, interests and expertise of individuals who might be interested in helping. Some jobs will require initiative and drive; others will be more behind the scenes.

Some roles will suit people with strong interpersonal skills; others will draw people with technical expertise. Ask people to do a specific job, and tell them why you see them as qualified. The team might include parish nurses, lay visitors, trainers, coordinators, someone with computer skills, an artist to design appropriate Scripture cards, a writer to compose newsletter articles, a group of retirees to lick stamps and stuff envelopes, and someone who enjoys keeping track of birthdays and significant anniversaries to send cards.

You might also want to think about involving Sunday-school teachers and their classes. For instance, at Christmastime our primary classes made cards for all the hospitalized or homebound church members and collected baskets of personal items for each. The junior-high students made manger scenes out of clothespins and shoe boxes. Most of those manger scenes are still sitting by the bedsides of the recipients, who continue to rave about them.

Another example occurred at a nurses' Bible study. Teresa, who worked in a suburban hospital, told of a patient she had been praying with for several days. "He told me that he's terrified because he is being transferred to a teaching hospital for bypass surgery and won't have anyone to pray with him there when he *really* needs it," she related to the group.

Evelyn perked up immediately, saying that she worked in the cardiac care unit at that hospital and would be delighted to pray with him. The group discussion turned to considering how they could develop a formal system for referring patients who needed spiritual care when transferred to other area hospitals.

"What we really need is a referral coordinator," someone suggested. The group determined that this person would need to be home most of the time, enjoy making phone calls and be organized enough to keep accurate records. Pauline, a retired nurse in the group, responded immediately. She mentioned that she had been looking for a way to continue her involvement in nursing and serve the group. Several group members spoke up at once, asking Pauline if she would coordinate the program.

Developing a lay visitor program in a church requires a lot of planning and organization. Let's say that you are interested in starting one in your church. The following steps will assure a solid foundation.

1. Find one or two others who share your interest in starting such a program. Give people the option to say no without feeling that they have let you down. You want people who really feel called by God, not who feel coerced. Meet first to pray. Your first meeting should probably be only for prayer and searching the Scriptures for guidance. As you become convinced of the need and God's direction, you will be ready to start thinking about who and what will be involved. For instance, you will obviously need lay visitors, but you will also need the blessing and cooperation of the church leadership, a coordinator, secretarial help, trainers and resource people, an educational program, a place to meet, a budget and funding (yes, even volunteer programs need money for training, paper, postage and supplies).

2. *Meet with the pastor* to share your ideas. Be humble. Ask for advice. If the pastor tells you that the idea has already been tried but didn't work, ask to hear more about what happened. Be prepared to explain how you would handle potential problems (such as lack of interest, inadequate support from the board, inappropriate behavior of volunteers or complaints from those visited). Ask about church policies and procedures for beginning such a ministry. Work within the system, even if it seems cumbersome and time-consuming—it will work to your advantage in the long run. A sure way to guarantee antagonism (and failure) is to defiantly implement a program without full support of the pastor and board of deacons or elders.

3. *Gather information.* Assess your congregation's needs using the guidelines in chapter two. Visit other churches with a similar program. Ask how they got started, how they are organized and if they have suggestions for you. Find out about existing training programs and other resources. You may want to link up with a national program with professional training and materials, or you might decide to develop your own approach. Your denomination

may provide the help you need. Look in Christian bookstores for books and study guides. New ones are appearing every day. After examining your options, decide on a plan and include it in your budget.

4. Begin to recruit volunteers. Invite each one to do a specific job, explaining why you see him or her as well suited for that role. Be clear about the time commitment required, including training and preparation, as well as the actual ministry involvement. Again, be sure you give each person the option of saying no without feeling guilty. Set a limit on the commitment, with the option to renew, so the volunteer doesn't feel it must be a lifetime obligation.

Communicating the Vision

Once your volunteers are on board, the key to keeping them is to communicate the vision for ministry. If people feel that their services are needed and appreciated, they will be eager to invest the time and energy required—even when the going gets tough. If they are doing the job only because they feel coerced or shamed into it, they will be half-hearted volunteers. Guilt is a poor motivator; vision inspires. Vision enables people to see the good and gives meaning to their work. Vision can be shared, but then it must be owned by the other person in order to be effective. The process of vision-building creates excitement and stirs passion.

The Scriptures provide insights into God's vision for our ministry. For instance, a group of nursing students was studying Matthew 25 and became convicted that God wanted them involved with serving the poor. They began to volunteer at a homeless shelter, where they did everything from washing dirty feet and serving meals to leading worship services and praying with individuals. Their Bible studies then turned to examining how Jesus ministered to people, and they began asking, "What would Jesus do?"

in regard to the real-life situations they were facing.

Telling stories communicates vision on an ongoing basis. As volunteers at a food shelter told friends the stories of those they served, the number of volunteers steadily increased. My own congregation supported the food pantry by collecting canned goods on a regular basis, but with a poor response. Then we invited the directors of the pantry to speak to the congregation. They told of children from our own community whose eyes lit up upon seeing even a bag of generic cookies—and who left the pantry hugging the bag.

They also vividly related the downward spiral of another family who came to the pantry. The mother was dying of breast cancer. The father, an engineer, had been suddenly laid off from his job when his company lost a government contract, leaving him not only without an income but with no health insurance. Their entire savings were wiped out by medical expenses. They had managed to pay the mortgage on their home by working odd jobs, but just barely. The volunteers began by meeting the family's physical needs, providing food, finding school bags and shoes for the children, and finding someone to stay with the mother and children while the father looked for work. They also began meeting their spiritual needs, praying with them and eventually drawing them into a church community.

Hearing these stories brought the congregation to tears and to a new sense of commitment. They felt compassion for these very real people. The pile of donated food got a lot larger! And giving became an act of true caring, not just a guilt-inspired duty.

However, vision is more than an emotional response. A vision that motivates and sustains commitment needs to be clearly focused and fairly concrete. Two different kinds of vision for a lay visitor program might be "reaching our community for Christ" and "encouraging our homebound members." The former would require outgoing volunteers who enjoy meeting new people and stepping boldly into unknown situations. The latter would suit someone who enjoys more intimate, long-term relationships. Both vision statements are clearly focused and measurable. But these are two different ministries.

Other vehicles for communicating vision include writing articles about the ministry for a church newsletter, a denominational magazine or even the local paper. Local papers look for interesting community events and services to cover. You can share your vision and your stories with a reporter who will write the article for you. Not only will your own volunteers be thrilled with seeing themselves and their ministry in print (often with photographs), but others in the community may catch the vision as well.

If you feel comfortable with public speaking, you can volunteer to share your vision at area pastoral associations, senior citizen groups or interest groups in other churches. I am currently spreading the vision for parish nursing to churches in my area. First I spoke at the local interdenominational ministerial meeting. Then calls started coming from those pastors, inviting me to speak to the nurses in their congregations. Programs began in seven of those churches. Now I am speaking to other ministerial groups, teaching spiritual care at our local hospital and encouraging parish nurses in the community. A warning here: Spreading the vision may create more new opportunities than you can handle, so be prepared to set priorities.

Training Others to Care
Once you have communicated the vision, you will begin with a group of enthusiastic volunteers. Parish nursing is a good example. The idea has caught on like wildfire. Nurses around the world

have caught the vision. Nurses who are dissatisfied with the impersonal managed-care approach often see parish nursing as "what I always wanted to do." Retired nurses frequently see parish nursing as a way to continue in a profession they loved.

A caution: Well-intentioned but untrained volunteers may do more harm than good. Parish nursing requires a deep understanding of the faith-health connection, up-to-date nursing knowledge and skills in spiritual care and community assessment. As I began to meet with parish nurses, I heard stories that raised grave concern. Some of these nurses were so rusty in their nursing skills that they were missing serious signs and symptoms. They had no idea how or where to refer people for help. They did not know how to meet spiritual needs and often turned to inappropriate alternatives. Now I am working with others in my community and denomination, as well as with Nurses Christian Fellowship, to educate volunteer parish nurses.

Training programs for volunteers can take several forms. An intensive orientation is a good way to start. The program might last one day or a week, depending on the complexity of the job. Elements to include in an orientation include the following:

☐ a statement of the biblical basis of the ministry

☐ the mission and beliefs of the particular church or organization providing the ministry

☐ an overview of how the ministry functions, including its history

☐ a clear job description

☐ resources available to do the job

☐ procedures for reporting and accountability

☐ an assessment of participants' needs and desires for continuing education and support

Training programs for adult volunteers must meet felt needs in order to be successful. To some extent you will want to allow the group to set the agenda, but you will also need to provide structure and resources. Beginning with the job description provides some specific areas to cover. Let's say that the job description for lay visitors in your church reads, "Lay visitors will call on the seriously ill and/or homebound members of the congregation in order to extend spiritual care and companionship."

The first concern to arise will probably be the mechanics of the visit. *What do I do and say? How often should I go? How long should I stay?* Generate some discussion by asking participants to share their experiences in visiting sick people, both positive and negative. Most will have positive experiences to share, or they wouldn't be volunteering now, but others may raise concerns and fears. The discussion will give you clues about possible topics to offer in the training program. Let's listen in on a possible interaction:

Mary: I went to deliver the sermon videotape to Louella last week. Louella is not a talker, and sometimes I get the feeling that she'd rather not have any visitors. But she looked so lonely, I asked if we could watch the tape together. She really lit up! After the tape was over, she talked and talked, and we prayed together.

Lester: I wouldn't know what to do if someone asked me to pray out loud. That just wasn't something I grew up with. People in this group seem so free about just talking to God like a good buddy, but I always thought you had to talk to God like you were talking to a king.

Bob: I feel the same way, but I think I'd like to learn how to pray more naturally.

Nancy: Well, I went to see Katherine yesterday, and all I could do was pray—for myself as well as her! She was in such misery. I don't understand why God allows her to suffer so. I feel guilty going in there all healthy and busy about life, while she lies there with only the four walls. She can't even get up in a chair anymore. I didn't know what to say, so I stayed about five minutes and left.

Mildred: When my mother was dying there was one dear woman who came to see her every day. She never said much; she just brought her knitting and sat with Mom for an hour or so. Sometimes she held her hand or told her little tidbits of news, but usually, she just sat there. Mom always looked forward to Emma's visits. I guess just *being there* speaks as loudly as words at a time like that.

Some clear themes have begun to emerge in this conversation. Participants are concerned about the mechanics of visitation. They seem to want help on how to conduct themselves during a home visit, especially if the person they are visiting doesn't talk or appear to welcome their presence. Some are concerned about the form and substance of prayer and how to pray with others. Concern about suffering and death surfaced. At the same time, some potential mentors are becoming apparent. Mary showed some creativity in her visit with Louella and seemed to move easily into conversation and prayer. Perhaps she could be teamed up with Lester or Bob. Mildred has learned the value of presence from personal experience. Maybe she could go with Nancy the next time she visits Katherine. It also appears evident that this group would welcome a course on how to provide spiritual care.

The next step is to determine the most effective type of learning for your group. Groups such as Nurses Christian Fellowship, Hospital Christian Fellowship, parish-nurse support groups, Christian Medical and Dental Society, Stephen Ministers and some denominational groups offer various programs for health care professionals and for lay visitors. Attending such a program will not only provide an organized approach and solid content but will also foster networking with others and inspire participants with a bigger vision. This tends to break through the "we've never done it this way" objections.

For instance, when Janice tried to encourage lay visitors to pray with those they visited, several women in the group insisted, "It's just not Lutheran to do that! Prayer is a private matter." Then they attended a denominationally sponsored prayer conference that encouraged conversational prayer. Now they felt permission to try it. Before long they had not only begun praying with others but even organized a weekly prayer group and an emergency prayer chain in the church.

Outside speakers who come to your group to present a program or lead a course will often be seen as more credible and authoritative than you or a member of your group. Asking someone from another church or a ministry organization to speak to your group will often expand their vision and increase the possibilities for ministry. For example, we recently had two speakers from a multichurch ministry that serves homebound people in the community. They shared their vision, told stories and explained their needs. Several of our church members volunteered to help and began attending a monthly volunteers' support group. They now bring ideas and challenges back to our own congregation.

Providing a regular opportunity for participants in your program to study Scripture together, share experiences and encourage one another will serve as an ongoing form of learning. As participants share, be alert for ways to reinforce principles already covered, and attempt to discern needs for further help. For instance, at one meeting several members began to discuss how they could "cheer up" two individuals who appeared clinically depressed. They were frustrated by weeks of unsuccessful attempts. "After all," one woman decreed, "depression is a sin; real

Christians should be joyful." They decided to invite a Christian counselor to speak to the group about the dynamics of depression and how to support those who were depressed.

Further possibilities for training programs include book discussions and Bible studies. Excellent new training materials are constantly being produced, in addition to those listed in the bibliography that follows this chapter.

Encouraging the Faithful

"You can't give what you don't got," the saying goes. You don't have to have a seminary education or know all the answers to tough questions to meet spiritual needs. You *do* need a vital relationship with God and a willingness to share that with others. Whenever you work with people, there will be times when you are misunderstood, unappreciated and even abused. We are sinners working with sinners. Don't be surprised when difficulties arise.

When we are volunteering in a church or Christian ministry, conflict usually catches us by surprise. We are easily tempted to withdraw to our corners and sulk—or try to get even. Interestingly, the Bible deals with conflict head-on. Jesus' disciples fought over which of them was the greatest (Mk 9:34). Paul got into a tiff with Peter (Gal 2), confronting him about his hypocrisy. Apparently Paul was so disappointed in John Mark that he refused to let him go along to Antioch (Acts 15:38). The New Testament Epistles make frequent references to squabbles among the believers, including a disagreement between Euodia and Syntyche that needed third-party mediation (Phil 4:2).

The Bible makes it clear that conflict is inevitable but that we need to deal with it and get on with ministry. Hebrews exhorts us, "Therefore lift your drooping hands and strengthen your weak knees, and make straight paths for your feet, so that what is lame may not be put out of joint, but rather be healed. Pursue peace with everyone, and the holiness without which no one will see the Lord. See to it that no one fails to obtain the grace of God; that no root of bitterness springs up and causes trouble, and through it many become defiled" (Heb 12:12-15).

Pursuing peace does not mean that we pretend the conflict doesn't exist or that we capitulate whenever someone disagrees. It does require us to hear out our opponents, then forgive them and love them, even if we disagree. Serving in Christ's name is more important than protecting our pride.

We don't have to build a case for our position; we should not foster discord by passing on bitter feelings and angry thoughts. Peter tells us, "Finally, all of you, have unity of spirit, sympathy, love for one another, a tender heart, and a humble mind" (1 Pet 3:8). And Paul exhorts, "Therefore encourage one another and build up each other" (1 Thess 5:11).

How can we build each other up? The letter to the Hebrews provides some guidelines: "Let us hold fast to the confession of our hope without wavering, for he who has promised is faithful. And let us consider how to provoke one another to love and good deeds, not neglecting to meet together, as is the habit of some, but encouraging one another" (Heb 10:23-25).

First, we need to keep our eyes focused on Jesus, whom we have confessed as our hope. When we are each trying to follow and serve Jesus, we will eventually end up walking in the same direction. And when we find ourselves facing constant suffering, death and failure, we can still know that Jesus has promised to be faithful. Our work is not in vain. Because we must be grounded in this hope in order to minister in Christ's name, our meetings should include Bible study, prayer and worship.

Second, we need to meet together to encourage one another in love and good works. Acknowledge the things others are doing well, struggle with them through their failures, pray for each other. Be vulnerable. Share your own joys and struggles. When you feel tempted to stay home and put your feet up instead of attending the support group meeting, remember that your absence is discouraging to the others. We need each other.

God has extended to us the privilege of ministering in his name. Caring for the spiritual needs of others allows us to tread on holy ground; we enter into partnership with the God of the universe. While the world around us seeks to tear down and destroy, the Lord has appointed us as agents of reconciliation as he builds his kingdom in our midst. This work is a wonderful and eternal investment.

Notes

Chapter 1: Spirituality & Health
[1]This particular assessment guide was recommended as preparation for a visiting prayer ministry. While most spiritual assessment guides do not include such lists of occult practices, perhaps they should. About half of the members of this congregation who completed the assessment guide indicated that they had tried various occult practices. Almost all of them were sensing some sort of continuing negative effects from these experiences. They probably would never have mentioned them if not asked directly.

[2]Matt Nisbet, "New Poll Points to Increase in Paranormal Belief," <http://www.csicop.org/articles/poll/index.html>.

[3]Richard Morin, "Can We Believe in Polls About God?" *Washington Post*, June 1, 1998, <http://washingtonpost.com/wp-srv/politics/polls/wat/archive/wat060198 .htm>.

Chapter 2: Assessing Spiritual Needs
[1]Adapted from Ruth I. Stoll in Judith Allen Shelly and Sharon Fish, *Spiritual Care: The Nurse's Role* (Downers Grove, Ill.: InterVarsity Press, 1988), p. 64.

Chapter 6: Prayer
[1]Daniel C. DeArment, "Prayer and the Dying Patient: A Way of Intimacy Without Exposure," *Princeton Seminary Bulletin* 66, no. 2 (summer 1974): 55.

[2]Ibid., p. 56.

Chapter 8: The Power of Touch
[1]Ashley Montagu, *Touching: The Human Significance of the Skin* (New York: Columbia University Press, 1971), pp. 82-84.

[2]Michael E. Phillips, "Appropriate Affection," *Leadership* 9, no. 1 (winter 1988): 110.

[3]Ibid., pp. 109-11.

[4]Lori Rentzel, *Emotional Dependency* (Downers Grove, Ill.: InterVarsity Press, 1990), pp. 22-28.

[5]For example, Fred DiCostanzo, "Complementary Care Flows into the Main-

stream," *The Nursing Spectrum* 3, no. 23 (1994): 3. See also Sandy Brasili, "Recovering the Mind-Body Connection: Diversity in Nursing Care," *The Scarab* (publication of the Medical College of Virginia Alumni Association) 45, no. 2 (spring 1996): 7-12. The popular media, including *Time, Life, Ladies Home Journal* and most local newspapers, have also reported heavily on Therapeutic Touch and other energy-based therapies.

[6]One nurse's terrifying story can be found in Sharon Beekmann, *Enticed by the Light* (Grand Rapids, Mich.: Zondervan, 1997).

[7]Elizabeth L. Hillstrom, *Testing the Spirits* (Downers Grove, Ill.: InterVarsity Press, 1995), p. 132.

[8]Richard J. Foster, *Prayer: Finding the Heart's True Home* (San Francisco: HarperSanFrancisco, 1992), p. 149.

[9]Sharon Fish, "Therapeutic Touch: Can We Trust the Data?" *Journal of Christian Nursing* 10, no. 3 (summer 1993): 6-7.

[10]Hillstrom, *Testing the Spirits*, pp. 118-19. Also see Marilyn T. Oberst, "Editorial: Our Naked Emperor," *Research in Nursing & Health*, 18 (1995): 1-2; Judith A. Turner et al., "The Importance of Placebo Effects in Pain Treatment and Research," *JAMA* 271 (May 1994): 1609-14; Deane H. Shapiro Jr., "Adverse Effect of Meditation: A Preliminary Investigation of Long-Term Meditators," *International Journal of Psychosomatics* 29 (1992): 62-66; Rochelle B. Mackey, "Discover the Healing Power of Therapeutic Touch," *American Journal of Nursing* 95, no. 4 (1995).

[11]In Mackey, "Discover the Healing Power," p. 29, the author describes an incident where she performed Therapeutic Touch on an unconscious patient. Many nurses who practice Therapeutic Touch have told me that they do not usually inform patients but practice the technique on patients who are asleep or unconscious.

[12]The laying on of hands first appears in the Old Testament, where it was commonly used to confer a blessing (see Gen 48:14). In the New Testament the laying on of hands by anyone other than Jesus (see Mk 5:23; 6:5; Lk 13:13) was used primarily for the ordination of church leaders or in connection with the gift of the Holy Spirit (see Acts 6:5-6; 8:18; 13:3; 19:6). Acts 28:8 is one exception, where Paul uses the laying on of hands for healing. In Acts 4:30 the disciples pray assuming that God is stretching forth *his* hand to heal. The practice of physically touching a person while praying for healing has continued throughout church history and been incorporated into the liturgies of many Christian traditions. The relationship of the person laying on hands is one of petitioner, not channeler or manipulator.

[13]Marty Kaplan, *Time*, June 24, 1996, p. 62.

Chapter 9: The Family Caregiver

[1]Linda L. Treloar, "Lessons from Joy: Living with Disability," *Journal of Chris-*

tian Nursing 15, no. 2 (spring 1998): 11.

[2]A ministry of BCM International (USA), 237 Fairfield Ave., Upper Darby, PA 19082, phone (610) 352-7177; BCM International (Canada) Inc., 798 Main Street East, Hamilton, Ont. L8M 1L4.

JAF Ministries, P.O. Box 3333, Agoura Hills, CA 91301, provides retreats and other resources for families dealing with disability. The JAF Ministries website provides a listing of other camps available for people with disabilities: <http://www.jafministries.com/helps/needhelp.htm>.

[3]For more information, contact Nurses Christian Fellowship, P.O. Box 7895, Madison, WI 53707-7895; phone: (608) 274-4823, extension 402; e-mail: ncf@ivcf.org; Web site: <http://www.ncf-jcn.org>.

[4]Stephen Ministries, 2045 Innerbelt Business Center Dr., St. Louis, MO 63114-5765; phone: (314) 428-2600; Web site: <http://www.stephenministry.org/>.

Chapter 10: Caring for Yourself
[1]See note 3 in chapter 9.

Further Reading

Bakken, Kenneth L., and Kathleen H. Hofeller. *The Journey Toward Wholeness: A Christ-Centered Approach to Health and Healing.* New York: Crossroad, 1988.

Biddle, Perry H., Jr. *A Hospital Visitation Manual.* Grand Rapids, Mich.: Eerdmans, 1994.

Carson, Verna Benner. *Spiritual Dimensions of Nursing Practice.* Philadelphia: W. B. Saunders, 1989.

Fish, Sharon. *Alzheimer's: Caring for Your Loved One, Caring for Yourself.* Carol Stream, Ill.: Harold Shaw, 1996.

Fitchett, George. *Assessing Spiritual Needs: A Guide for Caregivers.* Minneapolis: Fortress, 1993.

Haugk, Kenneth C. *Christian Caregiving: A Way of Life.* Minneapolis: Augsburg Fortress, 1985.

Matthews, Dale A., with Connie Clark. *The Faith Factor: Proof of the Healing Power of Prayer.* New York: Viking, 1998.

Miller, James A., Jr. *The Caregiver's Book: Caring for Another, Caring for Yourself.* Minneapolis: Augsburg Fortress, 1996.

O'Brien, Mary Elizabeth. *Spirituality in Nursing: Standing on Holy Ground.* Boston: Jones & Bartlett, 1999.

Phillips, Susan S., and Patricia Benner. *The Crisis of Care: Affirming and Restoring Caring Practices in the Helping Professions.* Washington, D.C.: Georgetown University Press, 1994.

Raber, Ann, ed. *A Life of Wholeness.* Scottdale, Penn.: Herald, 1993.

Richards, Larry, and Paul Johnson. *Death and the Caring Community: Ministering to the Terminally Ill.* Portland, Ore.: Multnomah, 1980.

Robbins, Jerry K. *Carevision: The Why and How of Christian Caregiving.* Valley Forge, Penn.: Judson, 1993.

Shelly, Judith Allen, and Arlene B. Miller. *Called to Care: A Christian Theology of Nursing.* Downers Grove, Ill.: InterVarsity Press, 1999.

Shelly, Judith Allen, and Sandra D. John. *Spiritual Dimensions of Mental Health.* Downers Grove, Ill.: InterVarsity Press, 1983.

Shelly, Judith Allen. *Spiritual Needs of Children*. Downers Grove, Ill.: InterVarsity Press, 1982.

Solari-Twadell, Phyllis Ann, and Mary Ann McDermott. *Parish Nursing: Promoting Whole-Person Health Within Faith Communities*. Thousand Oaks, Calif.: Sage, 1999.

Wangerin, Walter, Jr. *Mourning into Dancing*. Grand Rapids, Mich.: Zondervan, 1992.

Westberg, Granger E., and Jill Westberg McNamara. *The Parish Nurse: Providing a Minister of Health in Your Congregation*. Minneapolis: Fortress, 1990.

Resources Available from Nurses Christian Fellowship

P.O. Box 7895, Madison, WI 53707-7895
(608) 274-4823, ext. 402
ncf@ivcf.org

NCF Bible Study Guides

1. Colossian Capsules Twenty brief studies that cover the entire letter to the Colossians. Appropriate for personal or small group Bible study. Looks at "Establishing a Christian Identity," "Christian Living in the World," "Preparing for Ministry" and "Doing the Work," with five studies in each of the four sections.

2. Following Christ in Nursing Six studies from the Gospels, which identify principles demonstrated by Jesus Christ in relating to people. Topics include "Offering Peace to People Facing Death," "Communicating Forgiveness" and "Comforting Relatives Experiencing Grief."

3. Lifestyle of Joy Seven studies from Philippians focus on how we can reflect Jesus Christ in nursing. Studies include "Joy in Serving," "Rejoicing in the Lord" and "Joy in Living and Dying."

4. Lifestyle of Love Christ summarizes a lifestyle of love in John 13—17. These seven studies highlight the priorities Christ had for the disciples as he launched them into the world. This guide applies these priorities to our work in a secular context.

5. Living in Hope Hope is like love—a feeling. But more than that, hope is seen in actions that reflect what is inside a person. Eight studies include "Our Living Hope," "Hope—Where Do You Find It?" "Hope—Based on the Character of God" and "Grieve, But with Hope."

6. Mental Health: A Biblical Perspective Eight studies looking at various aspects of this definition of mental health: "A state of dynamic equilibrium characterized by hope, joy, love and peace where relationship with God, self, others and the world around are mediated by the love of God and wherein one experiences the peace of God about the past, present and future."

7. Walking in the Light Twelve studies designed to help us *be* and *live* as Christ's people in the world and assist us in understanding and growing in forgiveness.

8. Walking Through the Valley Twelve studies designed to provide a balanced biblical view of suffering and healing as well as a scriptural perspective on death and dying. One objective is to help nurses learn to communicate God's love and care to those facing suffering and death and to their families.

Caring People Series

1. Handbook for Caring People How can I help those who are hurting all around me? This handbook provides simple time-tested principles for dealing with the pain people feel. Each chapter has questions that can be the basis for a small group discussion.

2. Caring for Emotional Needs Nine studies that help you understand what emotional health can mean personally and for those for whom you care.

3. Caring for People in Conflict Nine studies that help to show how God can bring healing and reconciliation in the lives of those around you as well as in your own life.

4. Caring for People in Grief These nine studies help us consider fear, peace, grace, hope, comfort and more. There is a way to provide genuine comfort to those who are grieving.

5. Caring for Physical Needs God cares about our physical needs. When we care for the needs of others we are showing God's care. These eight studies will explore this important aspect of Christian ministry. In addition to learning to care for others, you will also learn how God cares for you.

6. Caring for Spiritual Needs Nine studies that will help you learn how to meet spiritual needs in your life and in the lives of others.

7. The Character of Caring People These eight studies will show you how to focus on the gifts of caring which God has given you—such as hospitality, generosity and encouragement.

8. Resources for Caring People These eight studies focus on resources such as Scripture, prayer, the Holy Spirit, listening and acceptance, which will help you meet the needs of other people.

Other NCF Publications

1. Concepts in Nursing—A Christian Perspective Editor Ruth Stoll. How does believing and living out biblical concepts affect nursing practice? Which of these concepts are crucial in order to care for others as Christ did? This book gives some beginning answers to these questions. Written by an NCF task force on spirituality, the concepts are: value of the person, relationship, communion, servanthood, stewardship, health and community. Each chapter ends with a clinical example and discussion questions.

2. Writing for Publication: Influencing Your Profession for Jesus Christ Have you wanted to write an article for a nursing journal, but didn't know where to begin?

Judith Allen Shelly gives step-by-step guidelines in this easy-to-use guide. Tested in writers' workshops across the United States, even those who thought they could not write have produced articles for publication using this guide. Contains text, worksheets and reference charts in a loose-leaf notebook so you can add your own notes and manuscript drafts.

3. *Teaching Spiritual Care* A resource book for nursing faculty who want to teach spiritual care in the nursing curriculum. Includes eight paradigms from secular and Christian schools of nursing and gives clear examples of what can be done. Each program or course reflects varied concerns and philosophies. In all eight situations, the spiritual care content has been enthusiastically received by students and supported by the school's faculty and administration.

4. *This We Believe—About Life and Its Value* (pamphlet)

5. *This We Believe—About Suffering* (pamphlet)

6. *A Response to Energy-based Theories and Therapies* (pamphlet) How Christians respond to Therapeutic Touch and other energy-based therapies in a way that is both sensitive and faithful.